PAIDAMOYO PHILLIPA JACKSON

Shattered Dreams

HOW POLITICAL AND ECONOMIC
HARDSHIP HAS DISPLACED A WHOLE
PEOPLE IN ZIMBABWE

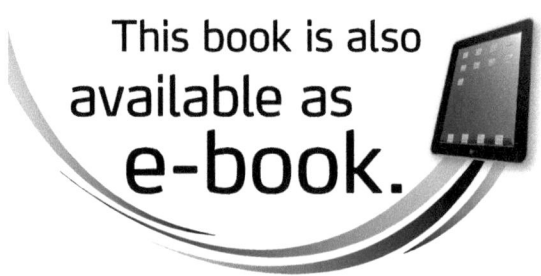

www.novum-publishing.co.uk

All rights of distribution, including via film, radio, and television, photomechanical reproduction, audio storage media, electronic data storage media, and the reprinting of portions of text, are reserved. Printed in the European Union on environmentally friendly, chlorine- and acid-free paper.	© 2017 novum publishing ISBN 978-3-99064-017-3 Editing: Rachel Jones, BA Cover photo: Natanael Alfredo Nemanita Ginting | Dreamstime.com Cover design, layout & typesetting: novum publishing **www.novum-publishing.co.uk**

CONTENTS

Book 1
Pre-Rhodesian Period 12

Book 2
Rhodesian Period 44

Book 3
Zimbabwean period 76

I DEDICATE THIS BOOK TO MY MOTHER AND LATE FATHER WHO MADE ME WHO I AM

ACKNOWLEDGEMENT

I would like to extend my appreciation to: Everyone who took their time to proof read and help compile this book, and also to those who gave me the courage to write this book. You know yourselves, God bless you all, and I will never thank you enough, you will always be in my thoughts.

INTRODUCTION

Inasmuch as these are my lifetime experiences, I felt compelled to write my research on the history of my country Zimbabwe and share it with you. We all dream! When we are sad, we dream of a future filled with happiness. When the weather is cold and wet, we dream of warm days when the sun always shines. When we feel unwell we dream of being healthy and strong all our lives. When we are broke we dream of a future full of money, never mind where the money is going to come from! In addition, of course we dream of winning millions in the lottery and being able to shop until we drop.

Nowadays in my country Zimbabwe, most ordinary people dream of things that people in the developed world take for granted – for example, being able to buy food, clothing and having a roof over their heads. Most people dream of being able to get a job so they can pay school fees for their children, pay for healthcare and look after their families and their extended families. Right at the back of their minds, they may dream of a day when they could afford luxuries like cars, electricity and telephones. These are dreams that they know will never come true in their lives. They stay in the very far unreachable distance.

Indeed, there was a time when life in my country Zimbabwe was easier as long as one worked hard, dreams used to come true. These are the so called 'good old days!' anyone, even the street vendors, could afford to pay for all the basic necessities of life plus a few more luxuries like big stereos, televisions and even cars. Other professionals like teachers and nurses could easily afford to buy houses in the suburban areas. Most households could afford to employ nannies, house cleaners, chefs and gardeners. In fact, all of this we took for granted.

I, like everyone else, had some dreams. As a young girl I dreamt of getting married to the richest man I could find. That is because in the old days women were expected to get married, have babies and become housewives, I did not want to be selling fruits and vegetables at the market like my mother. In my teens, my dreams changed, I pushed the marriage dream to the further end of my twenties. I realised that if I worked hard enough at school I could do better than just getting married and producing babies. I decided that I wanted to become a professional model. I got this idea from the 'Parade' magazine and other international magazines. Towards the end of my high school years, my dreams changed. This was because of the promises of a better Zimbabwe where there would be better opportunities for all. I now dreamt of a profession in the financial institutions.

I dreamt of one day becoming an executive in the banking sector or even owning my own bank. Some years later, after working in one of the leading banks in the country, I discovered that my dream of being a banking executive let alone owning a bank was unachievable so my dreams changed. I left the country for Europe for a profession that would help me contribute to the development of the country. I thought this was a more challenging profession and that I could at least help my people. In fact, I decided that this was my final and last dream that promised the brightest and most exciting future that I had dreamt about for years and years. I was finally going to achieve my dreams!

Whatever dreams I had had from when I was a little girl to when I became a young woman, they were all about being successful in whatever profession I would choose to pursue. One thing that I never dreamt of was leaving my country to settle in a foreign country with uncertain future! I never dreamt of working as a care giver in an old people's home! I never dreamt of working in a hospital, let alone in a foreign country! My dreams have been shattered!

Blessed are those who have been able to achieve their dreams! In my country, people no longer 'dream!' they are too frightened of getting disappointed because dreams never come true. They just carry on their lives living each day as it comes. They have lost all hope for a brighter future. In fact, if they dream at all they always have nightmares about prices of basic items going up, dream about being beaten up by the police and about what other nightmares the government is planning for them! As for me, I have given up dreaming! There is no point of dreaming anymore because I have no idea what the future holds for me. I am too afraid of dreaming. I just thank God that I am alive and can at least put food on my table every day.

As far as this book is concerned, it details the hidden stories of Zimbabweans, regardless of colour, race or creed, living across the world away from our beloved country Zimbabwe. In any event, I never dreamt of politics, economic hardships to displace a whole people. My experiences have shown me however, that its perhaps not surprising, and I have come to realise that in a split second, one can become homeless, with nothing to live on, and a refugee in another country. I call them disasters, and these disasters are not natural, either or neither nor uncontrollable. We have learned the hard way, there are two disasters both of them can cause a very hard impact on human nature. There are manmade disasters, which in certain instances can be avoidable; these are due to economic, political, and power hungry. I call them disasters because it is very sad in the cruel inhumane means that one endures to hang on to power certainly Zimbabwe has shown those disasters, which have lacked the respect for human dignity, life has become abnormal. History, of course, can demonstrate many such instances throughout the whole of Africa and the globe. How easily people can become trapped in their our naivety – trusting people – believing that success is in the palms of their hands when – in reality – it is out of reach, due to political and economic circumstances. One quickly learns from bitter experience that bureaucracy and corruption can lead to the suffering, hunger of a given society. In this case, there are certain issues that in life you cannot avoid talking about one can no longer pretend that they are not affected. Heard that saying, "half the world is composed of people who have something to say and cannot, and the other half, those who have nothing to say, they keep on saying it"? Some of us are not part of the nothing to say brigade, which is the main reason I have written this book. I have suffered in silence long enough I suppose!

This book is based on a true story – the lifetime journey of an African woman – me. This is a woman's lifetime journey from Rhodesia to Zimbabwe and beyond. I was born in Rhodesia, in the deep African townships; I have a lot of township experience, growing up under the Rhodesian regime. I understand too well from first-hand experience the words 'racism' and 'segregation'.

Growing up in African townships where there was a lot of intimidation, beating, and people being arrested for no apparent reason. Fathers and mothers were beaten, humiliated in front of their children. The other issue that I will never forget was when there were demonstrations by African people staging their demonstrations by the town centre, Salisbury. The Rhodesian Police forces, Police Reserves and police guard dogs would be unleashed by the police chief commissioner into the townships to come and collect black Africans from whichever township they choose for arresting or beating individually. The questioning will be based on who are the leaders of the African parties, and did they participate in the planning and staging of the demonstrations. These people included children. That is when I experienced the collection of black people from their townships, when I was very young. When I was young and understood my surrounding, I swam in sewage water with my mother and sister. Following these childhood experiences there is a link to why a lot of people migrated abroad and other neighbouring countries. Most people including me migrating out of Zimbabwe was the last solution. It's been a life saviour and being able to live a normal life. As for those families that we left behind, life is bearable because of the financial support they are getting from us abroad.

In addition, if that means, leaving hearth and home – abandoning all you hold dear to work in another country – that is what people have to do; there was no alternative. That is what countless others and I had to do. Moreover, believe me we have wept bitter tears in the process, of leaving your beloved country and start a new life in an unknown world.

BOOK 1

PRE-RHODESIAN PERIOD

Following my adventurous research of my country Zimbabwe, I have looked for information about my country. I have read and collected information about the first British missionary explorers who discovered my country according to the history. Formerly Rhodesia, I have come to understand that Rhodesia was named after Cecil Rhodes, the British empire-builder who was one of the most important figures in British expansion into southern Africa, and who obtained mineral rights in 1888 from the most powerful local traditional leaders through treaties such as the Rudd Concession and the Moffatt Treaty signed by King Lobengula of the Ndebele. When Lobengula discovered later what the Rudd Concession really meant, it was too late. He satisfied himself by putting to death the councillors who had supported it and attempted to undermine the concession by granting a parallel one to a German prospector the following year – the so-called Lippert Concession.

Rhodesia then was illustrated as to form part of the great Central African plateau, and it consisted of one broad swelling plane, which is cutup and intersected by numerous rivers and streams. This plane, however, gives way in places to rocky moan, tams and valleys, some of the latter being of great beauty; while the famous Victoria Falls, in the west of the country, it seems as though the plateau itself had been ripped apart by some gigantic convulsion of nature.

Southern Rhodesia was divided into two great provinces: Mashonaland and Matabeleland, both of which were, in the main, well suited for colonisation and were without doubt destined to play an important part in the future history of the empire to which they belong. It was the former province that the first to attract the attention of prospectors and settlers, but it has been Matebeland that has, chiefly to the greater facilities in the way of transport and suchlike that it possessed, assumed the greater importance today; though, as soon as Mashonaland receives the same aids to its development, there was no reason to suppose that it will be one which was behind either Matebeland in minerals wealth or agricultural value, the two factors in the rapid opening up of a colony.

During this time the inhabitants of the vast country known as Rhodesia were the Mashonas and the Makalangas, who as African aboriginal tribes were quiet and inoffensive. They were extremely unwarlike, but were very clever workers in iron, which they obtained in quantities from the bases of some mountains, and deft in weaving the coarse grass that grew around them into mats for coverings; but it was for cattle raisers that they excelled. After the departure of the Portuguese they lived on, quietly and in peace, until about 1840, when a terrible Black Horse, meaning Zulu Warriors, swept across the country, carrying death and desolation for all who opposed it, and causing the timorous owners of the soil to flee to the hills and other inaccessible spots, in much the same fashion as the Saxon and Danish freebooters drove the ancient Britons into the rocky fastness of Wales.

This invading force was a branch of the terrible and warlike Zulu tribe under the leadership of Mizilikazi, a cruel and despotic chief, and the tribe under him soon became famous as the Matabele. The Zulus had for ages occupied the whole of the country where the Transvaal and the Orange Free State are now situated. The tribe was constantly fighting or "washing their spears" as they euphemistically termed it, but when the Boers took the field against them they found that they met more than their match. Their heroic spear charges were of but little avail with opponents that contented themselves with lying behind rocks and pouring volleys of rifle fire into them, while their shields of skins, too, were of but small avail in stopping the bullets. They therefore retreated into the north of the republic and settled on the shores of the Limpopo River, but they were soon at war again.

The Mashona and Makalanga tribes could offer but little resistance to these redoubtable warriors, and were driven before them like chaff before wind. The Matabele length settled down beyond the Matopos hills, and such of the original inhabitants as escaped the general massacres that took place were driven to seek refuge in the mountains near Zambezi, where they built their villages on top of in accessible crags, and dwelt in constant fear of their bloodthirsty neighbours until the arrival of the British ten years later, and the subsequent crushing of the Matabele power, when they were once more able to come down to the plains and work in peace and without going daily dread of extermination. Rhodes and Rudd also used deceit, assuring Lobengula that no more than ten white men would mine in Matabeleland, but this was left out of the actual document Lobengula signed. Furthermore it stated that the mining companies could do anything necessary for their operations. In the months of negotiations, Rhodes also used Dr. Leander Starr Jameson, whom Lobengula regarded as his friend having previously been treated by him for gout, to help persuade him. However, Rhodes managed to buy out Lippert.

Great Zimbabwe is a ruined city that was once the capital of the Kingdom of Zimbabwe, which existed from approximately 1100 to 1400 during the country's Late Iron Age. The monument, which first began to be constructed in the 11th century and which continued to be built until the 14th century, spanned an area of 722 hectares (1,784 acres) and at its peak could have housed up to 18,000 people. Great Zimbabwe acted as a royal palace for the Zimbabwean monarch and would have been used as the seat of their political power. One of its most prominent features was its walls, some of which were over five metres high and which were constructed without mortar. Eventually the city was largely abandoned and fell into ruin. The ruins were first encountered by Europeans in the late 19th century with investigation of the site starting in 1871 The monument caused great controversy amongst the archaeological world, with political pressure being put upon archaeologists by the government of Rhodesia to deny its construction by black peoples. Great Zimbabwe has since been adopted as a national monument by the Zimbabwean government, with the modern state being named after it. The word "Great" distinguishes the site from the many hundreds of small ruins, known as Zimbabwe's, spread across the Zimbabwe Highveld. There are 200 such sites in southern Africa, such as Bumbusi in Zimbabwe and Manyikeni in Mozambique, with monumental, mortar less walls and Great Zimbabwe is the largest.

The ruins form three distinct architectural groups. They are known as the Hill Complex, the Valley Complex and the Great Enclosure. The Hill Complex is the oldest, and was occupied from the ninth to thirteenth centuries. The Great Enclosure was occupied from the thirteenth to fifteenth centuries and the Valley Complex from the fourteenth to sixteenth centuries. Notable features of the Hill Complex include the Eastern Enclosure, in which it is thought the Zimbabwe Birds stood, a high balcony enclosure overlooking the Eastern Enclosure, and a huge boulder in a shape similar to that of the Zimbabwe Bird. The Great Enclosure is composed of an inner wall, encircling a series of structures and a younger outer wall. The Conical Tower, 18 feet (5.5m) in diameter and 30 feet (9.1m) high, was constructed between the two walls. The Valley Complex is divided into the Upper and Lower Valley Ruins, with different periods of occupation.

There are different archaeological interpretations of these groupings. It has been suggested that the complexes represent the work of successive kings: some of the new rulers founded a new residence. The focus of power moved from the Hill Complex in the twelfth century, to the Great Enclosure, the Upper Valley and finally the Lower Valley in the early sixteenth century. The alternative "structuralism" interpretation holds that the different complexes had different functions: the Hill Complex as a temple, the Valley complex was for the citizens, and the Great Enclosure was used by the king. Structures that were more elaborate were probably built for the kings, although it has been argued that the dating of finds in the complexes does not support this interpretation. Some researchers have presented an argument that the ruins may have housed an astronomy observatory, although the significance of the alignments upon which these claims are based is contested.

ZAMBEZI EXPEDITION BY DAVID LIVINGSTONE

David Livingstone (19 March 1813–1 May 1873) was a Scottish Congregationalist pioneer medical missionary with the London Missionary Society and an explorer in Africa. In May 1873 David Livingstone, the celebrated missionary-explorer, died at Ilala, in the unknown heart of the continent, and his sun-dried body was brought home to be buried in Westminster Abbey. From his brass-plated tomb under the nave, Livingstone sounded a call for a worldwide crusade to open up Africa. A slave trade, organised by the people and Arabs in east Africa, was eating out the heart of the continent. Livingstone's answer was the '3Cs': Commerce, Christianity and Civilisation, a triple alliance of Mammon, God and social progress. Trade, not the gun, would liberate Africa. Perhaps one of the most popular national heroes of the late 19th century in Victorian Britain, Livingstone had a mythic status, which operated on a number of interconnected levels: that of Protestant missionary martyr, that of working-class "rags to riches" inspirational story, that of scientific investigator and explorer, that of imperial reformer, anti-slavery crusader, and advocate of commercial empire.

The men who followed David Livingstone out to Africa and scrambled greedily for their share are now half-forgotten. In their days they were famous and infamous feted as heroes, denounced as brutes and humbugs. There were journalist-explorers like Henry Stanley, sailor explorer like Pierre de Brazza, soldier explorers like Fredrick Lugard, pedagogue-explorers like Carl Peters, gold and diamond tycoons like Cecil Rhodes.

David Livingstone's fame as an explorer helped drive forward the obsession with discovering the sources of the River Nile that formed the culmination of the classic period of European geographical discovery and colonial penetration of the African continent. At the same time his missionary travels, "disappearance" and death in Africa, and subsequent glorification as posthumous national hero in 1874 led to the founding of several major central African Christian missionary initiatives carried forward in the era of the European "Scramble for Africa".

The British government agreed to fund Livingstone's idea and he returned to Africa as head of the Zambezi Expedition to examine the natural resources of South-eastern Africa and open up the River Zambezi. Unfortunately it turned out to be completely impassable to boats past the Cabora Bassa rapids, a series of cataracts and rapids that Livingstone had failed to explore on his earlier travels. The expedition lasted from March 1858 until the middle of 1864. Expedition members recorded that Livingstone was an inept leader incapable of managing a large-scale project. He was also said to be secretive, self-righteous, moody and could not tolerate criticism which severely strained the expedition and which led to his physician, John Kirk, writing in 1862, *"I can come to no other conclusion than that Doctor Livingstone is out of his mind and a most unsafe leader"*.

The expedition became the first to reach Lake Malawi and they explored it in a four-oared gig. In 1862 they returned to the coast to await the arrival of a steam boat specially designed to sail on Lake Malawi. Mary Livingstone also arrived along with the boat. She died on 27 April 1862 of malaria and Livingstone continued his explorations. Attempts to navigate the Ruvuma River failed because of the continual fouling of the paddle wheels from the bodies thrown in the river by slave traders, and Livingstone's assistants gradually died or left him. It was at this point that he uttered his most famous quote, "I am prepared to go anywhere, provided it is forward." He eventually returned home in 1864 after the government ordered the recall of the expedition because of its increasing costs and failure to find a navigable route to the interior. The Zambezi Expedition was castigated as a failure in many newspapers of the time, and Livingstone experienced great difficulty in raising funds further to explore Africa. Nevertheless, the scientists appointed to work under Livingstone, John Kirk, Charles Meller, and Richard Thornton did contribute large collections of botanic, ecological, geological and ethnographic material to scientific Institutions in the United Kingdom. David Livingstone died in that area in Chief Chitambo's village at Ilala southeast of Lake Bangweulu in present-day Zambia on 1 May 1873 from malaria and internal bleeding caused by dysentery. He took his final breaths while kneeling in prayer at his bedside. (His journal indicates that the date of his death would have been 1 May, but his attendants noted the date as 4 May, which they carved on a tree and later reported; this is the date on his grave.) Britain wanted the body to give it a proper ceremony, but the tribe would not give his body to them. Finally they relented, but cut the heart out and put a note on the body that said, "You can have his body, but his heart belongs in Africa!" Livingstone's heart was buried under an Mvula tree near the spot where he died, now the site of the Livingstone Memorial. His body together with his journal was carried over a thousand miles by his loyal attendants Chuma and Susi to the coast to Bagamoyo, and was returned to Britain for burial.

CECIL RHODES

Cecil John Rhodes was born on 5 July 1853 in the small hamlet of Bishop's Stortford, England. He was the fifth son of Francis William Rhodes and his second wife, Louisa Peacock. A priest of the Church of England, his father served as curate of Brentwood Essex for fifteen years, until 1849, when he became the vicar of Bishop's Stortford, where he remained until 1876. Rhodes had nine brothers and two sisters and attended the grammar school at Bishop's Stortford. When he was growing up Rhodes read voraciously but vicariously, his favourite book being *The Meditations* by Marcus Aurelius, but he equally adored the highly esteemed historian Edward Gibbon and his works on the great Roman Empire. Rhodes fell ill shortly after leaving school and, as his lungs were affected, it was decided that he should visit his brother, Herbert, who had recently immigrated to Natal. It was also believed, by both Rhodes and his father that the business opportunities offered in South Africa would be able to provide Rhodes with a more promising future than staying in England. At the tender age of 17 Rhodes arrived in Durban on 1 September 1870. He brought with him three thousand pounds that his aunt had lent him and used it to invest in diamond diggings in Kimberley.

After a brief stay with the Surveyor-General of Natal, Doctor P. C. Sutherland, in Pietermaritzburg, Rhodes joined his brother on his cotton farm in the Umkomaas valley in Natal. By the time Rhodes arrived at the farm his brother had already left the farm to travel 650 kilometres north, to the diamond fields in Kimberley. Left on his own Rhodes began to work his brother's farm, growing and selling its cotton, proving himself to be an astute businessman despite his young age. Cotton farming was not Rhodes' passion and the diamond mines beckoned. At 18, in October 1871, Rhodes left the Natal colony to follow his brother to the diamond fields of Kimberley. In Kimberley he supervised the working of his brother's claim and speculated on his behalf. Among his associates in the early days were John X Merriman and Charles D. Rudd, of the infamous Rudd Concession, who later became his partner in the De Beers Mining Company and the British South Africa Company.

In 1872 Rhodes suffered a slight heart attack. Partly to recuperate, but also to investigate the prospects of finding gold in the interior, the Rhodes brothers trekked north by ox wagon. Their trek took them along the missionary road in Bechuanaland as far north as Mafeking, then eastwards through the Transvaal as far as the Murchison range. The journey inspired a love of the country in Rhodes and marked the beginning of his interest in the road to the north and the northern interior itself.

In 1873 Rhodes left his diamond fields in the care of his partner, Rudd, and sailed for England to complete his studies. He was admitted to Oriel College Oxford, but only stayed for one term in 1873 and only returned for his second term in 1876. He was greatly influenced by John Ruskin's inaugural lecture at Oxford, which reinforced his own attachment to the cause of

British Imperialism. Among his Oxford associates were Rochford Maguire, later a fellow of All Souls and a director of the British South Africa Company, and Charles Metcalfe. At university Rhodes was also taken up with the idea of creating a 'secret society' of British men who would be able to lead the world, and spread to all corners of the globe the spirit of the Englishman that Rhodes so admired. He wrote of this society,

Why should we not form a secret society with but one object the furtherance of the British Empire and the bringing of the whole uncivilised world under British rule for the recovery of the United States for the making the Anglo-Saxon race but one Empire.'

His university career engendered in Rhodes his admiration for the Oxford 'system' which was eventually to mature in his scholarship scheme: 'Wherever you turn your eye – except in science – an Oxford man is at the top of the tree'.

AN ARCH IMPERIALIST

One of Rhodes' guiding principles throughout his life, that underpinned almost all of his actions, was his firm belief that the Englishman was the greatest human specimen in the world and that his rule would be a benefit to all. Rhodes was the ultimate imperialist, he believed, above all else, in the glory of the British Empire and the superiority of the Englishman and British Rule, and saw it as his God given task to expand the Empire, not only for the good of that Empire, but, as he believed, for the good of all peoples over whom she would rule. At the age of 24 he had already shared this vision with his fellows in a tiny shack in a mining town in Kimberley, when he told them,

'The object of which I intend to devote my life is the defence and extension of the British Empire. I think that object a worthy one because the British Empire stands for the protection of all the inhabitants of a country in life, liberty, property, fair play and happiness and it is the greatest platform the world has ever seen for these purposes and for human enjoyment'.

A few months later, in a confession written at Oxford in 1877, Rhodes articulated this same imperial vision, but with words that clearly showed his disdain for the people whom the British Empire should rule:

"I contend that we are the first race in the world, and that the more of the world we inhabit the better it is for the human race. Just fancy those parts that are at present inhabited by the most despicable specimen of human being, what an alteration there would be in them if they were brought under Anglo-Saxon influence ... if there be a God, I think that what he would like me to do is paint as much of the map of Africa British Red as possible ..."

One of Rhodes' greatest dreams was a ribbon of red, demarcating British territory, which would cross the whole of Africa, from South Africa to Egypt. Part of this vision was his desire to construct a Cape to Cairo railway, one of his most famous projects. It was this expansive vision of British Imperial control, and the great lengths that Rhodes went to in order to fulfil this vision, which led many of his contemporaries and his biographers to mark him as a great visionary and leader.

The fourth 'C' conquer Africa was introduced by Cecil John Rhodes. Rhodes was both ruthless and incredibly successful in his pursuit of this scheme of a great British Empire. His contemporaries marvelled both at his prowess and incredible energy and capacity, but they also shuddered at his callousness and depravity in all his pursuit. His contemporaries, both awed and appalled by the man, wrote of him as a man of original ideas who sought more than the mere 'getting and spending which limits the ambitions and lays waste the powers of the average man'. Yet although many people at the time saw Rhodes as a man of great vision, an unconquerable leader with the ability to pursue his aims across the vast African continent, there were nonetheless dissident voices who were shocked by Rhodes' actions and those of his British South Africa Company. One such voice was that of Olive Schreiner, who, initially awed by Rhodes, had come to abhor him. In April of 1897 she wrote, in a letter to her friend, John Merriman:

"We fight Rhodes because he means so much of oppression, injustice, & moral degradation to South Africa; – but if he passed away tomorrow there still remains the terrible fact that something in our society has formed the matrix which has fed, nourished, built up such a man!"

THE KING OF DIAMONDS

Whilst at Oxford, Rhodes continued to prosper in Kimberley. Before his departure for Oxford Rhodes had realised that the changing laws in the Kimberley area would force the 'small man' out of the diamond fields and would only leave larger companies able to operate in the mines. In light of this he sought to consolidate a number of mines with his partner, Charles Rudd. Rhodes had also decided to move away from the 'New Rush' Kimberley mine fields that were higher in the ground and thus more accessible, back to the lower yielding 'Old Rush' area. Here Rhodes and Rudd bought the costly claim of what was known as old De Beers (Vooruitzicht Farm) which owed its name to Johannes Nicolaas de Beer and his brother, Deidrick Arnoldus de Beer, the original owners of the farm Vooruitzicht. It was this farm that would lend its name to Rhodes and Rudd's ever growing Diamond Company.

In 1874 and 1875 the diamond fields were in the grip of depression, but Rhodes and Rudd were among those who stayed to consolidate their interests. They believed that diamonds would be numerous in the hard blue ground that had been exposed after the softer, yellow layer near the surface had been worked out. During this time the technical problem of clearing out the water that was flooding the mines became serious and he and Rudd obtained the contract for pumping the water out of the three main mines.

Rhodes had come to the realisation that the only way to avoid the cyclical boom and bust of the diamond industry was to have far greater control over the production and distribution of diamonds. And so, in April 1888, in search of an oligopoly over diamond production, Rhodes and Rudd launched the De Beers Consolidated Mines mining company. With 200 000 pounds capital the Company, of which Rhodes was secretary, owned the largest interest in mines in South Africa. Rhodes greatest coup was to get Barney Barnato, owner of the Kimberley mine, to go partnership with Rhodes' De Beers Company. Of the encounter Barnato later wrote:

"When you have been with him half an hour you not only agree with him, but come to believe you have always held his opinion. No one else in the world could have induced me to into this partnership. But Rhodes had an extraordinary ascendancy over men: he tied them up, as he ties up everybody. It is his way. You can't resist him; you must be with him."

With his acquisition of most of the world's diamond mines Rhodes became an incredibly rich man. But Rhodes was not after wealth for wealth's sake, he was acutely aware of the relationship between money and power, and it was power which he sought. Hans Sauer wrote of a conversation he had had with Rhodes whilst looking over the Kimberley diamond mine, where Sauer had asked Rhodes, 'what do you see here?', and, Sauer writes, 'with a slow sweep of his hand, Rhodes answered with the single word: "Power".

In the early 1880s gold was discovered in the Transvaal, sparking the Witwatersrand Gold Rush. Rhodes considered joining the rush to open gold mines in the region, but Rudd, convinced him that the Witwatersrand was merely the beginning, and that far greater gold fields lay to the north, in present day Zimbabwe and Zambia. As a result Rhodes held back while other Kimberley capitalists hastened to the Transvaal to stake the best claims. In 1887 when Rhodes finally did act and formed the Goldfields of South Africa Company with his brother Frank, most of the best claims were already taken. Goldfields South Africa performed very poorly, prompting Rhodes to look towards the north for the gold fields that Rudd had assured him were lying in wait.

THE STATESMAN

In 1880 Rhodes prepared to enter public life at the Cape. With the incorporation of Griqualand West into the Cape Colony in 1877 the area obtained six seats in the Cape House of Assembly. Rhodes chose the constituency of Barkley West, a rural constituency in which Boer voters predominated, and at age 29 was elected as its parliamentary representative. Barkley West remained faithful to Rhodes even after the Jameson Raid and he continued as its member until his death.

The chief preoccupation of the Cape Parliament when Rhodes became a member was the future of Basutoland, where the ministry of Sir Gordon Sprig was trying to restore order after a rebellion in 1880. The ministry had precipitated the revolt by applying its policy of disarmament to the Basuto. Seeking expansion to the north and with prospects of building his great dream of a Cape to Cairo railway, Rhodes persuaded Britain to establish a protectorate over Bechuanaland (now Botswana) in 1884, eventually leading to Britain annexing this territory.

Rhodes seemed to have immense influence in Parliament despite the fact that he was acknowledged to be a poor speaker, with a thin, high pitched voice, with little aptitude for oration and a poor physical presence. What made Rhodes nonetheless so incredibly convincing to his contemporaries has remained much of a mystery to his biographers?

THE PUSH FOR MASHONALAND

Rhodes' imperial vision for Africa was never far from his mind. In 1888 Rhodes looked further north towards Matabeleland and Mashonaland, in present day Zimbabwe. Matabeleland fell squarely in the territory which Rhodes hoped to conquer, from the Cape to Cairo, in the name of the British Empire. It also was believed to hold vast, untapped gold fields, which Rudd believed would be of far greater value than those discovered in the Witwatersrand.

In pursuit of his imperial dream and in his desire to make up for the failure of his Gold Fields Mining Company, Rhodes began to explore ways in which to exploit the mineral wealth of Matabeleland and Mashonaland. The King of Matabeleland, King Lobengula, who was believed by the British to also rule over Mashonaland, had already allowed a number of British miners' mineral rights in his kingdom. He had also sent a number of his men to labour in the diamond mines, thus setting precedence for engagement with him. However, the King had consistently stated quite clearly that he wanted no British interference in his own territory.

In 1887 Lobengula signed a treaty with the Transvaal Government, an act that convinced Rhodes that the Boer were trying to steal 'his north'. By this stage the 'scramble for Africa' was also already well under way and Rhodes became convinced that the Germans, French and Portuguese were going to try to take Matabeleland. These fears made Rhodes razzpidly mobilise in order to get Matabeleland under British control. Although the British government at the time was against further colonial expansion to the north of South Africa, Rhodes was able to use the threat of other imperial powers, such as Germany, taking over the land to push the British Government to take action.

The Government sent John Smith Moffatt, the then Assistant Commissioner to Sir Sidney Shippard in Bechuanaland (now Botswana) who was well known to the Matabele Chief Lobengula as their fathers were friends, to negotiate a treaty with Lobengula. The result was the Moffat Treaty of February 1888, essentially a relaxed British protection treaty. The Moffat Treaty was however between Lobengula and the British Government, Rhodes himself was hardly a relevant player in this. Worried that the Moffat Treaty was too weak to hold Matabeleland, and convinced that the Dutch and Germans were making plans to take the territory and desperate for exclusive mining rights in the region, Rhodes concocted to his own plan to take control of the territory. With his business partner Rudd, Rhodes formed the British South Africa Company (BSAC), crafted on the British and Dutch East India company models. The BSAC was a commercial-political entity aiming at exploiting economic resources and political power to advance British finance capital.

Shortly after the Moffat Treaty, in March 1888, Rhodes sent his business partner Charles Rudd to get Lobengula to sign an exclusive mining concession to the British South Africa Company. When Rudd arrived at Lobengula's kraal however, there were a number of other British concession hunters already there, seeking to undertake the exact same manoeuvre as Rhodes' BSAC. Through Rhodes influence however, Rudd was able to win over the support of the local British officials staying with Lobengula, a move which ultimately convinced Lobengula that Rudd had more power and influence than any of the other petitioners seeking concessions from him.

After much negotiation Rudd was eventually able to get Lobengula to sign a concession giving exclusive mining rights to the BSAC in exchange for protection against the Boer and neighbouring tribes. This concession became known as the Rudd Concession. Lobengula's young warriors were angry and inflamed and were itching to kill the white men who were entering their lands. Lobengula however feared his people would be defeated if they attacked the whites, and so it is likely that he signed the Rudd Concession in the hopes of gaining British protection and thereby preventing a Boer migration into his lands which would then incite his warriors to battle. For Lobengula his options were essentially to either concede to the British or to the Dutch. In the belief that he was protecting his interests he sided with the seemingly more lenient and liberal British. Like so many documents signed by Africans during the colonial period, the Rudd Concession was however not what it claimed to be, but rather became a justifying document for the colonisation of the Ndebele and the Shona.

Using the Rudd Concession, despite initial protests by the British Government, Rhodes managed to acquire a Royal Charter (approval from the British monarch) for his British South Africa Company. The Royal Charter allowed Rhodes to act on behalf of British interests in Matabeleland. It gave the company full imperial and colonial powers as it was allowed to create a police force, fly its own flag, construct roads, railways, telegraphs, engage in mining operations, settle on acquired territories and create financial institutions.

Rhodes convinced the British Government to give his company the right to control those parts of Matabeleland and Mashonaland that were 'not in use' by the African residents there and to provide 'protection' for the Africans on the land that was reserved for them. This proposal, which would cost the British taxpayer nothing but would extend the reaches of the British Empire, eventually found favour in London. The charter was officially granted on 29 October 1889. For Rhodes is BSAC with its Royal charter was the means whereby which to expand the British Empire, which a timid government and penurious British treasury were not about to accomplish.

After gaining his charter from the British Government, Rhodes and his compatriots in the BSAC essentially felt that Matabeleland and Mashonaland were now under their control. Rhodes felt that war with the Ndebele was inevitable and would not allow his plans for extending the British Empire to be thwarted by "a savage chief with about 8000 warriors". Rhodes was determined that white settlers would soon occupy Matabeleland and Mashonaland, and the Ndebele could not resist them.

To gain power over Matabeleland and Mashonaland Rhodes hired Frank Johnson and Maurice Heaney, two mercenaries, to raise a force of 500 white men who would support Bamma Ngwato, enemies of Lobengula's, in an attack on Lobengula's kraal. Johnson offered to deliver to Rhodes the Ndebele and Shona territory in nine month for £ 87,500. Johnson was joined by Frederick Selous, a hunter with professed close knowledge of Mashonaland. Rhodes advised Johnson to select as recruits primarily the sons of rich families, with the intention that, if the attack did fail and the British were captured, the British Government would be left with no choice but to send armed forces into Matabeleland to rescue the sons of Britain's elite. In the end Johnson's attack was called off because Rhodes had received news that Lobengula was going to allow Rhodes' men into Matabele and Mashonaland without any opposition.

Despite Lobengula capitulating and giving permission for vast numbers of BSAC miners to enter his territory, Rhodes calculated a new plan to gain power in the region. In 1890 Rhodes sent a 'Pioneer Column' into Mashonaland, a column consisting of around 192 prospecting miners and around 480 armed troopers of the newly formed British South Africa Company Police, who were ostensibly there to 'protect' the miners. By sending in this column, Rhodes had deviously planned a move which would either force Lobengula to attack the settlers and then be crushed, or force him to allow a vast military force to take seat in his country. In the words of Rutherford Harris, a compatriot of Rhodes:

"… if he attacks us, he is doomed, if he does not, his fangs will be drawn and the pressure of civilisation on all his border will press more and more heavily upon him, and the desired result, the disappearance of the Matabele as a power, if delayed is yet the more certain."

The men who formed part of the Pioneer Column were all promised both gold concessions and land if they were successful in settling in Mashonaland.

On 13 September 1890, a day after the Pioneer Column arrived in Mashonaland, Rhodes's BSAC invaded and occupied Mashonaland without any resistance from Lobengula. They settled at the site of what was later to become the town of Salisbury, present day Harare, marking the beginning of white settler occupation on the Zimbabwean plateau. They raised the Union Jack (the British national flag) in Salisbury, proclaiming it British territory.

The prospectors and the company had hoped to find a 'second Rand' from the ancient gold mines of the Mashona, but the gold had been worked out of the ground long before. After failing to find this perceived 'Second Rand', Rhodes, instead of allowing the settlers mining rights, as had been agreed to by Lobengula, granted farming land to settler pioneers, something which went expressly against the Rudd Concession.

THE END OF THE MATABELE

In conceding Mashonaland to the BSAC Lobengula had avoided going to war with the British and had kept his people alive, and much of his territory intact. But unfortunately he had only been able to delay the inevitable. With no gold was found in Mashonaland, Rhodes' BSAC was facing complete financial ruin. Leander Jameson suggested to Rhodes that 'getting Matabeleland open would give us a tremendous life in shares and everything else'. Gaining the Matabeleland territory would also play directly into Rhodes megalomaniac vision of expanding the British Empire across Africa.

And so, in 1893, the BSAC eventually clashed with the Ndebele, in what Rhodes had perceived as an inevitable war. The settlers justified their initial attacks against the Ndebele to the British Government by arguing that they were protecting the Shona against the 'vicious' and 'savage' Ndebele Impis. This was however a ploy, consciously conducted by Jameson in conjunction with Rhodes, in order to ensure that the British Government would not object to their further intrusions into Matabeleland by creating the impression that the Ndebele were the first aggressors. To fight their war the company recruited large bands of young mercenaries who were Promised Land and gold in exchange for their fighting power.

The final blow any hopes that the Ndebele might avoid war, came when Jameson was able to convince the British Government that Lobengula had sent a massive Impis of 7000 men into Mashonaland, who then gave Jameson leave to engage in defensive tactics. There is no indication that the Impis Jameson reported on had ever existed. Lobengula himself, in a last appeal to the legal/rational system the British seemed to so fervently uphold, wrote to the British High Commissioner saying, "Every day I hear from you reports which are nothing but lies. I am tired of hearing nothing but lies. What Impis of mine have your people seen and where do they come from? I know nothing of them."

It was however far too late for Lobengula. With the permission to engage in defensive action from the British Government

Rhodes joined Jameson in Matabeleland and his group of mercenary soldiers struck a quick and fatal blow at the Ndebele. Rhodes' mercenaries were in possession of the latest in munitions technology, carrying with them into the veld maxim guns, which, like machine guns, could fire rapid rounds. The Ndebele Impis were helpless in the face of this brutal killing technology and were slaughtered in their thousands. Lobengula himself realised he could not face the British in open combat and so he burnt down his own capital and fled with a few warriors. He is presumed to have died shortly afterwards in January of 1894 from ill health.

The war against the Matabele, fought mostly by voluntary mercenaries, cost around £ 66,000. Most of the money to pay for this war came directly from Rhodes Consolidated Goldfields Company, which by this point had begun to produce excellent yields from the deeper lying gold fields. The conquered lands were named Southern and Northern Rhodesia, to honour Rhodes. Today, these are the countries of Zimbabwe and Zambia. By the 1890s these conquered territories were being called Southern and Northern Rhodesia.

THE PRECURSOR TO APARTHEID

In July 1890 Rhodes became the Prime Minister of the Cape colony, after getting support from the English-speaking white and non-white voters and a number of Afrikaner-bond, whom he had offered shares in the British South Africa Company. One of Rhodes most notorious and infamous undertakings as Prime Minister in South Africa, was his institution of the Glen Grey Act, a document that is often seen as the blueprint for the Apartheid regime that was to come.

On 27 July 1894, Rhodes gave a rousing speech, full of arrogance and optimism, to the Parliament of Cape Town that lasted more than 100 minutes. In this speech Rhodes was opening debate on the 'Native' Bill that he had been working on for two years. The bill had initially been intended merely as an administrative act to bring more order to the overcrowded eastern Cape district of Glen Grey, but in his typical fashion Rhodes had turned this routine administrative task into something far bigger, the formulation of what he described as a 'Native Bill for Africa'. In much of his speech Rhodes set out, in clear cut terms, the chief purpose of his 'Native Bill', to force more Africans into the wage-labour market, a pursuit which would undoubtedly also help Rhodes in his own mining claims in Kimberley and the Transvaal.

Rhodes opened his speech on the Glen Grey Act with the following words:

'There is, I think, a general feeling that the natives are a distinct source of trouble and loss to the country. Now, I take a different view. When I see the labour troubles that are occurring in the United States, and when I see the troubles that are going to occur with the English people in their own country on the social question and the labour question, I feel rather glad that the labour question here is connected with the native question.'

He then continued,

'The proposition that I would wish to put to the House is this, that I do not feel that the fact of our having to live with the natives in this country is a reason for serious anxiety. In fact, I think the natives should be a source of great assistance to most of us. At any rate, if the whites maintain their position as the supreme race, the day may come when we shall all be thankful that we have the natives with us in their proper position ... I feel that I am responsible for about two millions of human beings. The question which has submitted itself to my mind with regard to the natives is this" What is their present state? I find that they are increasing enormously. I find that there are certain locations for them where, without any right or title to the land, they are herded together. They are multiplying to an enormous extent, and these locations are becoming too small ... The natives there are increasing at an enormous rate. The old diminutions by war and pestilence do not occur ... We have given them no share in the government "I think rightly, too" and no interest in the local development of their country. What one feels is that there are questions like bridges, roads, education, plantations of trees, and various local questions, to which the natives might devote themselves with good results. At present we give them nothing to do, because we have taken away their power of making war "an excellent pursuit in its way" which

once employed their minds ... We do not teach them the dignity of labour, and they simply loaf about in sloth and laziness. They never go out and work. This is what we have failed to consider with reference to our native population ... What I would like in regard to a native area is that there should be no white men in its midst. I hold that the natives should be apart from white men, and not mixed up with them ... The Government looks upon them as living in a native reserve, and desires to make the transfer and alienation of land as simple as possible ... We fail utterly when we put natives on an equality with ourselves. If we deal with them differently and say, "Yes, these people have their own ideas," and so on, then we are all right; but when once we depart from that position and put them on an equality with ourselves, we may give the matter up ... As to the question of voting, we say that the natives are in a sense citizens, but not altogether citizens "they are still children ..."

The Glen Grey Act was to pressure Africans to enter the labour market firstly by severely restricting African access to land and landownership rights so that they could not become owners of the means of production, and secondly by imposing a 10 shilling labour tax on all Africans who could not prove that they had been in 'bona fide' wage employment for at least three months in a year. This land shortage coupled with a tax for not engaging in wage labour would push thousands of Africans into the migrant labour market. These were all measures essentially designed to ensure a system of labour migration which would feed the mines in both Kimberley and the Rand with cheap migrant labour. This section of the act instigated the terrible migrant-labour system that was to be so destructive in 20th century South Africa.

Another pernicious outcome of the Glen Grey Act was its affected on African land rights claims and restricted and controlled where they could live. According to the act 'natives', as African peoples were then termed, were no longer allowed to sell land without the permission of the governor, nor where they allowed to divide or sublet the land or give it as inheritance to more than one heir. The act also laid out that the Glen Grey area and the Transkei should remain "purely native territories". This act was eventually to become the foundation of the 1913 Natives Land

Act, a precursor to much of the Apartheid policy of separate development and the creation of the Bantustans.

Lastly the Glen Grey Act radically reduced the voting franchise for Africans. One of Rhodes primary policies as Prime Minister was to aim for the creation of a South African Federation under the British flag. A unified South Africa was an incredibly important political goal for Rhodes, and so when the Afrikaner Bondsmen came to Rhodes to complain about the number and rise of propertied Africans, who were competing with the Afrikaners and characteristically voted for English, rather than Afrikaans, representative. In response to the Afrikaners' complaints, Rhodes decided to give them, in the Glen Grey Act, a policy which would disenfranchise the Africans competing with Afrikaners whilst also ensuring Africans could not own farms which would compete with the Afrikaners.

To disenfranchise Africans the Act raised the property requirements for the franchise and required each voter to be able to write his own name, address and occupation before being allowed to vote. This radically curtailed the number of Africans who could vote, essentially marking the beginning of the end for the African franchise. This new law allowed for the voter-less annexation of Pondoland. The Glen Grey Act also denied the vote to Africans from Pondoland no matter their education or property. Through the adoption of the Act, Rhodes managed to gradually persuade Parliament to abandon Britain's priceless nineteenth-century ideal that in principle all persons, irrespective of colour, were equal before the law.

The Glen Grey Act was vigorously opposed by the English speaking members of the Cape Parliament, but Rhodes, with his forceful character, was able to push the act through Parliament, and in August 1984 Rhodes' Glen Grey Act became law. The Glen Grey Act, which created the migrant labour system, formalised the 'native reserves' and removed the franchise of almost all Africans, is seen by many as lying the ground work for the Apartheid system of the 20th century.

THE FALL OF GIANTS

By 1895, at the height of his powers, Rhodes was the unquestioned master of South Africa, ruling over the destiny of the Cape and its white and African subjects, controlling nearly all of the world's diamonds and much of its gold, and effectively ruling over three colonial dependencies in the heart of Africa. Although Rhodes' policies were instrumental in the development of British imperial policies in South Africa, he did not, however, have direct political power over the Boer Republic of the Transvaal. He often disagreed with the Transvaal government's policies and felt he could use his money and his power to overthrow the Boer government and install a British colonial government supporting mine-owners' interests in its place. In 1895, Rhodes precipitated his own spectacular fall from power when he supported an attack on the Transvaal under the leadership of his old friend, Leander Jameson. It was a complete failure and Rhodes had to resign as Prime Minister of the Cape and head of the British South Africa Company in January 1896. After having befriended the Afrikaners for so many years, Rhodes' support of the Jameson Raidand his attempts to get the miners in Johannesburg to rise up in a coup against the leaders of the Transvaal, were seen by the Bondsmen and Afrikaners as a complete betrayal, and Rhodes' hopes of ever uniting South Africa under one flag were dashed against the rocks.

Despite his meteoric loss of power and prestige Rhodes nonetheless continued his political activities. In mid-1896 the Shona and Ndebele people in Southern Rhodesia, present day Zimbabwe, rose up against their colonial oppressors in a bid for freedom. Rhodes personally travelled to the region to take charge of the colonial response. In his attacks on the Ndebele and Shona he was vindictive, resorting to a scorched earth policy and destroying all their villages and crops.

After months of fighting Rhodes decided that conciliation was the only option. Looking to negotiate a peace settlement with the Ndebele and Shona he headed into the Matopo Mountains where a great indaba was held. Rhodes asked the chiefs why the Africans had risen up in war against the colonisers. The chiefs replied that the Africans had for decades been humiliated by the white settlers, subjected to police brutality and pushed into forced labour. Rhodes listened to the complaints and told the chiefs, "All that is over". The chiefs saw this as a promise that the conditions for them and their countrymen would be improved, and so they agreed with Rhodes that they would end their hostilities. As a part of their agreement Rhodes spent many days in the Matopo hills, and every day the Ndebele would come to him and voice all their complaints. In belief that their worries and complaints would be given just recognition, the Ndebele and Shona chiefs laid down their arms and returned to their fields. When he left Rhodes was lauded by the people whose suffering by the hands of colonists was only to increase in the next century, as the 'Umlamulanmkunzi', the peacemaker.

Thereafter, Rhodes was in ill-health, but he began concentrating on developing Rhodesia and especially in extending the railway, which he dreamed would one day reach Cairo, Egypt.

After the Anglo-Boer war that broke out in October 1899, Rhodes rushed to Kimberley to organise the defence of the town. However, his health was worsened by the siege, and after travelling to Europe he returned to the Cape in February 1902. He died on 26 March 1902 at Muizenberg in the Cape Colony (now Cape Town). Reportedly some of his last words were, 'so little done, so much to do'. Rhodes was buried at the Matopos Hills, Rhodesia (Zimbabwe). He left £ 6 million (approx. USD 960 million in 2015), most of which went to Oxford University to establish the Rhodes scholarships to provide places at Oxford for students from the United States, the British colonies, and Germany.

Rhodes never married and he did not have any known children and there is some suggestion that he was homosexual. This suggestion is based on the care and concern he showed to some men, but it is not enough to offer any solid truth.

* Blake, R. A. (1977) *A History of Rhodesia*. London: Eyre Methuen

POLITICAL STATUS OF RHODESIA

Rhodesia had limited democracy in the sense that it had the Westminster parliamentary system with multiple political parties contesting the seats in parliament, but as the voting was dominated by the white settler minority, and black Africans only had a minority level of representation at that time, it was regarded internationally as a racist state.

From 1899 to 1962 the Rhodesian Assembly comprised members elected to represent constituencies on a first past the post principle. At some stages, however, there were two-member constituencies, and in the early years there were some appointed members. The 1961 constitution adopted a more complex system intended to extend the franchise to wider sections of the community including non-whites – but without immediately bringing white rule to an end.

At the time of the Unilateral Declaration of Independence, Rhodesia's amended 1961 constitution (which was annexed to the UDI) provided for an Officer Administering the Government, to be appointed by the British Sovereign (or by the parliament if the Queen made no appointment), with political power residing with the unicameral Legislative Assembly.

Under the 1961 constitution, the Rhodesian Assembly had 65 elected members: 50 constituency members and 15 district members. The voter rolls had education, property and income qualifications. The main 'A' roll was for citizens who satisfied high standards in these regards and 95 % of its members were white and 5 % were black or Asian. The B roll had lower qualification standards and 90% of its members were black and 10% were white or Asian. The B roll was about one-tenth of the size of the A roll. Both rolls voted in elections for constituencies and districts, but for elections in the constituencies, the B roll vote was capped at 20% of the total, and for elections in the districts, the A roll vote was capped at 20% of the total. This procedure was known as 'cross-voting'. In practice, the 50 constituency members would all be white and the 15 district members would mostly be black.

The 1962 general election was a watershed for the country, since it resulted in the election of a Rhodesian Front government led by Winston Field that was committed to independence without majority rule and to the continued separate development of white and black communities in Rhodesia. The defeated United Federal Party led by Edgar Whitehead had been committed to slow progress to majority rule.

There was no explicit racial discrimination in the Rhodesian political system before 1969. It is sometimes claimed that had the black community participated more fully in the political process then the outcome of the 1962 general election would have been different and UDI would have been avoided. African nationalist groups objected to the 1961 constitution and urged those eligible to vote not to register, and those that had registered not to vote. Relatively few eligible Africans did register to vote, and B-roll voter turnout in the 1962 election was less than 25%.

The Rhodesians maintained the system was broadly fair since the 50/15 power share split reflected the relative contributions of white and black communities to the "fiscal" (that is, the tax take). Progress to black majority rule was possible within the arrangement of the 1961 constitution as a result of advances in black wealth and education, although it would have taken some years to achieve. It would have required the black community to patiently accept an extended period of white minority rule followed by an extended period of power sharing. Black politicians in the early 1960s were not minded to accept such an arrangement. In any event, income and property qualifications for the electoral roll had become an anachronism.

Ian Smith and other Rhodesians claimed that this political arrangement would have resulted in an evolutionary transition to black majority rule which would have avoided the rushed transition that had caused difficulty in other African countries. But critics maintain that the stubborn refusal to make immediate and visible progress to majority rule in the early 1960s set in train events which are causing serious trouble in modern Zimbabwe to this day (2005).

In 1965 there were revisions to the constitution that reflected the new status of the nation after UDI. Primarily, the revisions erased the rights of the British Government to legislate and act on behalf of Rhodesia, and provided for further constitutional amendments on a two-thirds majority of parliament. The Officer Administering the Government was to be the Commander-In-Chief of the Armed Forces.

1969 (UDI) CONSTITUTION

The Rhodesian Front government eventually drafted a completely new constitution. This further entrenched white minority rule and made the country a republic, following a referendum result in favour in 1969. Under this new constitution, there was a bicameral parliament consisting of an indirectly elected Senate, and a directly elected House of Assembly, in which the majority of seats were reserved for whites even more effectively than was the case under the 1961 constitution. The new office of president was a ceremonial post, with executive power remaining with the Prime Minister.

The 1969 constitution modified the detailed provision for electoral rolls and seats in the Assembly. The most significant 1969 modifications were that cross voting was abolished and the B roll was reserved for non-Europeans. The Assembly constituencies were reformed so that there were 50 A roll, and 8 B roll seats. It was provided that the number of B roll seats would rise over time in line with the proportion of total personal income tax paid by blacks until a total of 50 black seats was reached. In addition to the B roll seats, the African tribal chiefs were able to elect another 8 members. The immediate result of this arrangement was that 270,000 whites had 50 seats and 6 million Africans had 8 seats in the Assembly, with a handful of African chiefs having 8 seats as well. These reforms served only to reinforce black rejection of the system.

The new constitution gave a clear indication of where the architects of UDI thought Rhodesia should go in political terms. The concept of "separate development" for blacks and whites was written into that constitution. The concept of eventual parity of parliamentary representation between the races was also adopted. This last feature underpinned the concept of 'equal partnership between black and white' as an alternative to majority rule. However, the leaders of the UDI state made it clear that parity of representation could be deferred indefinitely, if not for ever. White immigration figures for the 1960s encouraged them to believe that it might be possible to significantly alter the demographic balance, given enough time.

The Rhodesian Front's victory in the 1962 general election and the subsequent UDI were in the populist tradition of Rhodesian politics. The early history of Rhodesian politics was very much one of electoral uprisings by miners, industrial workers and farmers against the big business establishment that dominated the colony. The election of the Reform Party government led by Godfrey Huggins in 1933 had a great deal in common with the RF win in 1962. It has been argued that the racial dimension of UDI was an incidental thing. Economic recessions in the early 1930s and the early 1960s had both produced the election of populist governments committed to securing standards of living for working people (albeit, the immediate concern was for working white people). It is significant that in the 1962 election, the RF recruited a slate of black candidates to contest the district (essentially B roll) seats. Those black Rhodesian Front candidates obtained little support from the B roll electorate and none were elected.

Rhodesia in the UDI era never quite took on the character of a one-party state. Although the Bush War was the real political contest, there was a conventional political opposition to the RF throughout the UDI period. The opposition came from white liberals who would contest A roll seats in general elections and from some black parties that would contest B roll seats. The main white opposition was the Rhodesia Party, associated with veteran liberal politician (and former district Assembly member) Dr Ahrn Palley. In the Rhodesia general election, 1974 Dr Palley came within 3 votes of taking Salisbury (City) from the RF. In that same election, Michael Auret took about 30% of the vote for the RP in Bulawayo (District). Auret later won Harare (Central) for the MDC in the Zimbabwe parliamentary elections, 2000. The RP did manage to secure around 20% of the white vote nationally on a regular basis and it would pick up most of the non-white constituency votes, but the first-past-the-post electoral system meant that they never won seats in the Assembly. Widespread press censorship and government control of radio and TV inhibited opposition activity. The lack of an effective parliamentary opposition is one factor that made it difficult to end UDI when this measure had become clearly necessary.

RP activists considered that most of their support came from the business elite, the professional class and from second or third generation Rhodesians. The more recent white immigrants tended to vote overwhelmingly for the RF. It has been suggested that Rhodesia hosted a peculiar brand of white politics traceable to British working-class immigrants who during the 20th century brought their successful struggle for a generous social welfare state out to the colonies. The RP group did not contest the 1977 general election because many of its activists had either been taken into one or other of various forms of detention or had been forced into exile. Michael Auret was expelled from Rhodesia in 1976 and told that he would be arrested immediately if he returned. Auret was unable to return home until 1980. The Rhodesian government was never tolerant of dissent throughout the UDI period, but it became positively repressive as the final debacle approached. The liberal former Prime Minister Garfield Todd and members of his family were subject to various forms of detention and house arrest.

The final political events in white Rhodesia were the 1977 general election and the 1979 referendum on extending equal voting rights to all citizens. An extreme right wing group known as the Rhodesian Action Party ('RAP') opposed the RF in the election and campaigned for a No vote in the referendum. The RAP group favoured a continuation of white minority rule and undertaking extreme military measures to win the Bush War. RAP attracted significant electoral support (15% of the referendum vote).

Some non-militant black groups and individuals contested and won B roll seats (often under the title "ANC Independent"). Under the 1969 constitution, the B roll was reserved exclusively for non-Europeans. This black political grouping was one of those that participated in the 1979 'internal settlement'. Association with the UDI state and with the internal settlement carried a collaborationist stigma that would damage the credibility of the black politicians involved.

THE END OF RHODESIA

When white minority rule was no longer tenable, Rhodesia moved first to a form of power sharing ('the internal settlement') and then to majority rule. At this point Rhodesia ceased to exist as a political entity and was replaced by Zimbabwe.

The end of UDI and of the Bush War was associated with an abrupt transfer of power to the insurgent backed, black political parties in 1980. Some observers feel that this resulted in some of the more stable elements in black civil society being marginalised. Consequently, Zimbabwe was not able to enjoy benefits of a managed transfer to democracy of the kind that took place in comparable neighbouring countries such as Botswana and South Africa.

BOOK 2

RHODESIAN PERIOD

START OF A JOURNEY

The Chinese say that a journey of a million miles begins with a single step. Well my journey of life began at an early age, when I started to understand my surroundings. Once upon a time, there was a country called Rhodesia, ruled by the British Empire. It became Zimbabwe ruled by the black majority people in 1980. I was born in Rhodesia and I grew up during the Rhodesian period until I was a young woman. During this period, black peoples' lives were ok for as long as you were working, had a roof over your head. However, as a black person there was always something about us that I started to realise when I was three years old. We were the low class. Coloured people had a better class than us. Coloured people were mostly in the Rhodesian army and most of the mixed race women were government clerks working in offices. Other coloured women were allowed to work in shops as shop assistants. They had their own dwelling areas, which had better living standards than the black Africans townships. Their dwelling areas were nearer to the town centres and nearer to the army barracks. They lived their life that was full of their own standards, fast cars, drinking until they drop, and big families.

As for the Indian people, they kept to themselves as different people from blacks and all other races in Zimbabwe. They had their arranged marriages. They never socialised that much with other people. They were trading and they are the ones who had paved their society's respect by offering their monies to buy land from the government to build their own houses out of town and away from the blacks, and nearer to the white Rhodesians. People of Indian origins were known for their business issues, and they never used the bank to bank their money that they accrued through their businesses. Indians were known to like black market business.

As for us black Africans, we had the option of becoming housekeepers, cleaners, (chamber-maids) hotel cleaners, gardeners, and all the dirty work you can think of. It was far too obvious there was no room for blacks. I remember in the Sixties when there were demonstrations by the black Africans of Rhodesia trying to liberate themselves from segregation, they wanted equal rights and opportunities, be offered to all besides colour race or creed with their fellow white Rhodesians. In the townships of Rhodesia, now Zimbabwe we used to have our supper around four o'clock in the afternoon and go to bed before six o'clock in the evening. 06:00pm to 06:00am curfew was imposed in our townships. After a demonstration in the town centre, there would be no rest in our town ships that night and the (BSAP) British South African Police will come to mobilise blacks and beat them up for the demonstration. I remember vividly, my young sister was around two years, and I was a three year old. My mother used to ask me to play with her whilst she prepared our meals; she used to bath us together in a big bath bowl as I used to call it.

On this particular day, people were forced out of our house late at night by the police reserves and frog marched to the police station by armed guards and guard dogs to be questioned, often beaten, torched and humiliated. We were collected to go to the nearest police station for my mother to be questioned, but my mother had other plans. We walked together with other people from our area. When we reached the small stream that was pouring sewage water into the sewage, my mother signed me to come with her swimming towards the sewage. We sat by this stream's banks in the reeds and there were bulldogs as well. If you were slow in walking the dogs would bite you. Thank god, my sister was so young and my mother was scared that she was going to cry. Nevertheless, fortunately, she never did, she was asleep, we sailed through the reeds, and we waited for the rest of people to go, we started crawling out of the stream. We went home and my mother gave us a cold bath and bathed herself as well, she couldn't warm the water, she was scared that maybe they might be other policemen who had remained still searching they would come, beat her up, since there was no human respect. She threw away all our clothes that we were wearing. The following day when my father returned home with my sister and brothers, he was very happy to see us all well and praised my mother; he said he knew she was going to make it. As we sat on my father's lap, together with my sister I could see the happiness in my father's eyes. That was the life in the African townships up and down, whilst we had a rest we, could hear that there was no rest in other township. We lived up to it, but it was hard. Talk of cuts and bruises; no one could talk about them besides just treat them quietly. It was as long as they are not life threatening. What did not treat the demonstration wounds salt, vinegar, barks of trees? People could not go to a hospital with these wounds, because they would be asked how they got wounded.

My mother laid us to sleep under the bed, because she was scared of the police officers who were left to check on the run away from the collected people. We were safe there under the bed. My mother is my hero; I love my mum she means the world to me. One thing that I remember mostly was the anger that we as children were exposed to, seeing their parents being humiliated and beaten, begging for mercy, the fact being this person is fighting for their human rights. Mostly, I think that is what made most of the young generation of blacks to go to war fight for freedom. That made children to hate white people. When I think of it, up to this day, these past political, discrimination situations that happened forty years ago still bring tears to my eyes. Some people survived the beatings, some were maimed for life, the so unlucky perished. It was clearly stated that people should, abide by the government rules, or keep quiet just go with the flow, or else you die that was the Rhodesian government law for blacks.

I grew up fearing the white people because there was no relationship between the black Africans, and white Rhodesians. The attitude of white people towards blacks was very bad. The racism was not hidden at all, you could easily see it if you visit a white area only place. The police would stop you and ask about what business you have in that areas. Since my father had access to go to the white only shops, I remember that he use to bring us chocolates from Woolworths which was a treat for the family. White Rhodesians use to call us names like, kefir. Blacks never used the front door; they used back door. Their jobs were cleaning and cooking and delivering mail using a bicycle from one point to the other. These messengers as they were called had a distinctive uniform of a khaki shirt and trousers. The shirts had a company logo printed on them, their pay was not very good, but they survived on it, since the living expenses were bearable.

When I started going to school, started understanding English, I remember walking in town reading some of the notices, in black and white, "No black people allowed in this shop" that limited blacks from getting into some shops. Whites had their own bus stops, their bus drivers were white as well, we had our own black bus drivers, bus stops, and we had our own toilets, which had a permanent stench emanating from, which could be smelt from a distance. Even by the town centre there were areas designated for blacks by the outskirts of the town Salisbury (now Harare). I remember each time when we would go shopping my mother would ask us to use the toilet before we leave home. I grew up thinking that the white people never go to the toilet the way we did, because of the superiority complex they showed us.

However, that never stopped us venturing into finding out why we were treated differently the anger grew inside as we grew older into adults. When I was much younger I never understood, why in our townships we lived had time restrictions and curfews, which restricted us from moving late at night and relatives visiting for as long as we wanted them to stay. When our relatives visit us, my parents had to take them to the police station in our township. At the police station, visitors were given an authorisation note with stipulated days allowed to visit. Because when the police patrol officers, do a random check they would ask for the household registration card. In case of an additional head they would request a note of authorisation stating number of days requested. In case of time elapse, you needed to renew it on the day of expiry. It was tough and rough.

That led to emergence of black African leaders to start organising and the recognition of the black people in the townships and mostly the martial laws and restrictions of movement. Due to the fact that our townships were monitored for any gathering, the leaders and their members decided to learn and practice whistling signals that their fellow leaders and members would interpret easily, whilst having meetings. Some of the whistling was an all-clear informing, the other whistling were alerting danger coming their way so that, they could switch off the light, or a paraffin lamp or to be quiet. Other whistling signals alerting the members not to movement, stay put or hide. Most of the houses had big hedges, bushy trees and flowers. The signal person was the most trusted, important person. The whistling communicators would mislead the police force patrolling in our townships at night, misguiding them to a different place all together so that others would quickly move from the danger area. It used to be three or more good whistlers. In the event failing to communicate with the next person, there would be some casualties people being beaten, maimed or arrested then they were sent to the famous, prison in Gwelo for political prisoners on a long term sentence. ("Gonakudzingwa" this prison was specifically built for political prisoners).

They had a way of communicating although there were no messaging systems that have come into play these days. I remember whistling was banned; if caught, whistling one could be arrested or beaten by the police if they suspected them as the night whistlers. This also made some of my nephews to be very vulnerable as they liked whistling at night just to provoke the police. Times were changing as I was growing up because black people realised that they were not free in their own motherland. There were loads of strikes and demonstrations and guerrilla warfare, the Rhodesian government realised that there was no going back for these blacks.

The government adjusted a number of its discriminatory laws, due to the fact that the gorilla war was starting to destabilize the country. The government removed the 06:00pm to 06:00am curfew in our townships; the night time police forces patrolling in our townships, their make shift police camp were also removed. All the signs that were discriminatory on the roads, shops, public places were removed. Africans were allowed to travel in the same buses as their fellow citizens white Rhodesians. The government announced on the radio and television that they wanted to have talks with the leaders of the black majority movement, in order to stop the war, and have a code of understanding between blacks and whites. The government requested all the African opposition parties to participate in the parliament elections, which were coming on that year. The black freedom fighters did not participate in those elections. To the government surprise, the freedom fighters party never participated. Nothing changed the war was still going on after the parliamentary elections.

Nevertheless, Muzorewa took over the new government of national unity, the country was renamed Zimbabwe Rhodesia and a new national flag was raised over Salisbury (now Harare), signifying the transition. It was expected that all sanctions would be lifted, now that the country was under democratically elected black majority rule. However, this did not lead to the lifting of sanctions as the hard-line parties ZAPU and ZANU were not involved in the political process. The British Government pressured Muzorewa to take part in the Lancaster House Conference in late 1979 in return for international recognition of the country and the lifting of sanctions. In March 1978, Smith and non-militant nationalist groups headed by Muzorewa, Sithole and Chief Jeremiah Chirau agreed what became the "Internal Settlement", under which the country would be reconstituted as Zimbabwe Rhodesia in June 1979 after multiracial elections. ZANU and ZAPU were invited to participate, but refused; Nkomo sardonically dubbed Smith's black colleagues "the blacksmiths". The deal was badly received abroad, partly because it kept the police, the military, the judiciary and the civil service in white hands. There would be a senate of 20 blacks and 10 whites, and whites would be reserved 28 out of 100 seats in the new House of Assembly. Smith and Nkomo re-entered negotiations in August 1978, but these ended after ZIPRA shot down an Air Rhodesia passenger flight on 3 September and massacred survivors at the crash site. Smith cut off talks, introduced martial law across most of the country and ordered reprisal attacks on guerrilla positions. Smith, Muzorewa and Sithole toured the US in October 1978 to promote their settlement, and met Kissinger, Ford and others including the future President Ronald Reagan. On 11 December, ZANLA attacked Salisbury's oil storage depot, causing a fire that lasted six days and destroyed a quarter of Rhodesia's fuel. Two months later ZIPRA downed another civilian flight, this time killing all on board.

After whites endorsed the Internal Settlement by 85% in a referendum on 30 January 1979, Smith dissolved the Rhodesian parliament for the last time on 28 February. The RF won all the white seats in the April 1979 elections while Muzorewa and the UANC won a majority in the common roll seats with 67% of the popular vote; the PF rejected this, however, as did the UN, which passed a resolution branding it a "sham". Sithole, astounded that his party had won only 12 seats to the UANC's 51, suddenly turned against the settlement and alleged that the polls had been stage-managed in Muzorewa's favour. Mugabe dismissed the bishop as a "neo-colonial puppet" and pledged to continue ZANLA's campaign "to the last man"; Nkomo similarly committed ZIPRA. On 1 June 1979, the day of the country's official reconstitution as Zimbabwe Rhodesia, Muzorewa replaced Smith as Prime Minister, at the head of a UANC–RF coalition Cabinet made up of 12 blacks and five whites. Smith was included as Minister without portfolio; Nkomo promptly dubbed him the "Minister with all the portfolios". What the African National Congress lead by Bishop Abel Muzorewa managed to change was better pay for black teachers.

The fact still remained that we had our own buses, bus stations. Township, shops, parks and entertainment centres. People lived their lives in their townships quietly, built, in the midst of air-polluted areas, recycled water which had a sewage smell. My mother use to boil the water again and again so that it could be used for drinking or cooking.

The first township to be built was called Harare, (Harare means, one who never sleeps) in this township people use to walk in the street day in day out. The police feared going into that township, due to people revolting towards police. It consisted of people of all occupations, but mostly, people working in the industrial areas. In big cities like Harare (then Salisbury), industries were springing up so labour was needed, just as well townships, like Highfield, Mabvuku, Tafara, Mufakose, and Kambuzuma were built.

At first, the government was against building houses for blacks even though they needed them to do all the hard work. They decided to build hostels where only men were allowed to live. These hostels were built within walking distance of the industrial sites. Their families had to stay back in the rural areas or Tribal Trust Lands (T.T.L's) as they called them. These hostels consisted of blocks of flats with single rooms, communal kitchens, bathrooms and toilets. Each room would house several men; wives were not allowed to visit their husbands.

Besides all this still some men used to smuggle their wives and girlfriend into the hostels but if they were caught they would be arrested, had to pay a fine then put on the buses back to their rural homes. Some would end up on the streets where they would be arrested again. It was a tough life for the black majority. Most men had to visit their families back in the rural areas on weekends or at the end of the month when they were paid. These hostels were becoming more and more overcrowded. Hygiene became a big problem because many people were sharing only a few bathrooms and toilets. There was also a permanent stench emanating from these hostels, which could be smelt from a distance.

These townships were strategically built in order for the industrialists to obtain cheap labour from the blacks who worked for next to nothing. They never considered that the pollution from smoke and the noise coming from the industries would be harmful to people's health. Some people suffered from unknown to African diseases. Every township had a police camp strategically build to control people's movement. Other black from Rhodesia by then were not interested in joining the police force or army. Firstly it was mostly people from (Fort Victoria) now Masvingo who were going for policing jobs and security guards, these were low class jobs. People hated them and use to call them, names, e.g. (BSAP) British South African Police, were called (BSAP) Broke Soon After Pay. On the other hand security guards were, chanted at, "if they beat you up, beat them back they are not police men", don't be afraid. Usually they used to work at night guarding building. Passers-by would laugh, shout and insult them. Night security guards with a guarding dog, people used to call them unspeakable names, some would ask how's your wife, meaning the guard dog. These guards were abused by the public, other people intentions were to provoke the guard so that they can break in the shop and steal. Policemen had respect from the society because they were law enforcers and protect people from the criminals.

RHODESIAN PERIOD

DECLARATION OF THE FEDERATION

The Declaration of the Federation (1969), for the migration of black people from Northern Rhodesia, Nyasaland was specifically meant to provide labour to the white farmers, industrial sector, and the mining sector of the country, Southern Rhodesia. Rhodesia had a high potential of the production of agricultural produce and mining of minerals, which had a high turnover on the international market that boosted the Rhodesian economy. The migration of black people within Northern Rhodesia, Nyasaland was immense due to people from these countries were looking for greener pastures. My grandfather was originally from Malawi. People from these countries were given work permits which they used to get to work in Rhodesia, which was called, "Chitikinyani", in a form of identification card. It consisted of a photo of the person, date of birth, nationality, job description, identity number and country of origin.

It also introduced intermarriages, because most of the migrant workers were young when they migrated from their countries. Most of the people working in towns were foreign migrant workers. Besides the industrialists, the other employer was the local council, which was responsible for providing sanitation to city dwellers. The sewage system was non-existent in the townships workers were responsible for collecting buckets full of excrement and garbage; these were mostly done by people from Malawi and Mozambique.

The foreign migrant worked in areas that locals didn't want to. Black migrant workers were also employed as domestic workers by most white families who provided them with accommodation in the back yard. These little houses were called 'boy's' kaya back yard cottage they were meant to be for single people. Most of them had no electricity. No visitors were allowed. When these workers were off duty they used to sit outside their bosses' gates, where they would meet other workers and socialise. If they had visitors, they would meet along the roadside, somewhere. It was indeed a tough life!

At first, all blacks were paid cash in hand by their employers. Blacks did not have bank accounts. As time went by the whites discovered that they were missing a lucrative business so they introduced a building society for blacks called the Central African Building Society. My father was one of the first people to open a savings account at this bank. My mother used to save my father's wages in an old tin for biscuits. My father bought a two bed roomed house in Highfield and we moved from the rural areas with him. These houses consisted of just the shell, with window frames; there were no window panes, no flooring and no doors inside. The finishing off was left for the buyer to do. Windows, people use to improvise and cover with plastic until they can afford to buy window panes. As for floors, they had to do the floors, either wood or cement mixture. The owner of the house had to look for a plaster specialist to do the floors and inside walls, which were not plastered as well. We were quite comfortable in our little house.

My father had it done before we came in to live in the house; he was a much organised person. The houses were allocated through the company employment contract, usually when one loses a job they had to vacate the house. The municipality of Harare, other major towns had to let people remain in their houses. Social services had supported the families of the foreign workers. Applications to the council were submitted by the allocated social worker for people to be allowed to stay in their houses even if they lost their jobs. Tenants in these houses were mostly Malawian, Zambian migrant workers and had no rural homes. This resulted in most houses in townships owned by Malawians not by the local people.

Workers also fought to be provided with larger houses for their growing families and the government allowed the local council to build more houses in the new townships of Glen Norah,

Chitungwiza and Glen View. The local council also allowed black people who already had houses to extend them. There was no electricity in our houses and there were no street light. People use to get home as early as they could before dark. We had a life, although not good enough. It was full of intimidation and laws were hard to abide to.

The Reserve Bank of Rhodesia's introduced banking services to black Africans as they realised that they were losing out on income from bank charges and mortgages interest rates. Most banks introduced mortgages, personal loans to all races. It came as a surprise since personal loans and mortgages were for whites and coloured people. Africans started receiving their wages through the banks and the post office bank, which started expanding into the rural areas. They had a lot of interesting Adverts on television as well as on big billboards which were being put anywhere strategically for people to see, especially on the roads from the African townships to the town centre. Also in the *The Herald* Newspaper there were pictures of African people advertising the banks some adverts were in the form of pamphlets which were distributed by helicopters, scattered from the air into the black townships. The post office was mostly used for sending money telegrams or a simple telegram for immigrants working in Rhodesia, especially Malawians, Zambians and Mozambique's to their relations back home.

For those who had settled, and managed to buy their own houses, the banks offered building loans for extensions or re-building houses. Many blacks took on these loans initially thinking they were attractive but they discovered they were still then paying 10-25 years later. People had to apply for an extension plan through the council. The council would send their surveyor to measure the stand and advise on how he would feel the extension should be carried. The final decision would take six to twelve weeks. After the approval of the new extension, building materials and labour were provided. The bank allocates the building contractors. When my father got the final drawing of our new house I remembered that he father refused to get a loan from the bank he preferred to buy bits and pieces until he was in a position to start rebuilding our house. It out that if he had to do it himself it was cheap no hassles for paying endless loans or being in danger of our house repossessed, or either sold to recover the loan. However, with the help of my mother selling vegetables, father working as a driver, our house was build within a year. I remember coming home to a new house which had a front room, dining room, bedrooms and a kitchen. Passer-bys and neighbours used to come around to see the progression of our new house, admiration. We were very happy to live in the house; we also had electricity for lighting, cooking, fridge and a television a house phone.

The rural areas (TTL) Tribal Trust Lands as they were called were not divided equally between Europeans and Africans of Rhodesia (18-million hectares of land). Yet there were roughly one hundred times as many African farmers as whites and African-designated land was almost exclusively in the regions with poorer soil (barren lands) and poor rainfalls.

An attempt to challenge the status quo by non-violent political methods was met with repression. In the early 1960s ZAPU and ZANU were banned and their leaders, detained without trial. In November 1965 the Rhodesian, government declared a State of Emergency, which gave it powers. On November 11, 1965, a few days after introducing the state of emergency, the Rhodesian Front government led by Ian Douglas Smith, made a (UDI) Unilateral Declaration of Independence from Britain, which signalled an increase in the repression of black nationalism and an end to any hope of peaceful constitutional reform, in the late 1960s the nationalist parties launched an armed struggle against the (technically illegal) Rhodesian regime, which from 1972 onwards developed into major bush war. The regime used increased brutal methods to suppress nationalist agitation. The scope of the death penalty was dramatically extended and there were dozens of secret executions of opponents. Torture was systematic and widespread, and included beatings, electric shocks and immersion in water until the victim lost consciousness. The introduction of the

Selous Scouts in the Matebeleland area by the Rhodesian government was to increase intimidation to the rural people, in the sense that they recruited black Africans to join them and pretend that everything was well and there was no war going on. Others were more of civilians (black Zimbabweans), wearing their day clothes and were used to secretly investigating the whereabouts of the freedoms fighters.

The security forces responded by indiscriminate measures against the rural population. Three quarters of a million rural Zimbabweans were moved into protected villages. The idea, which originated with the British in Malaysia, practiced by the United States in Vietnam, and has been followed by several other governments in devising counter insurgent strategies, was to isolate the civilian population from the guerrillas by forcing them to live in compounds. Villagers were forced to stay in the protected villages by strict dusk to dawn curfews. Curfew breakers were shot. Forced removals combined with the curfew meant that some could not reach their fields to cultivate. In the first year of protected villages in one area, deaths increased by 37%. Eighty% of these were from starvation and one in every five adults (let alone children, who were more vulnerable) suffered from malnutrition. Parallel with the protected villages' policy was "Operation Turkey," the army's ironic name for a policy of destroying food supplies in the rural areas. The ostensible aim was to allow only the barest minimum of food to reach the rural population so that they would have none to share with the guerrillas. The Rhodesian army burned down kraals and granaries, closed shops and grinding mills and shot cattle. The combined effect of the protected villages and Operation Turkey was to increase the demoralization and war weariness of the people and arguably, to create pressure on the leaders of the nationalist parties to accept less favourable terms for independence than they might otherwise have held out for. At independence, the outlying areas of Zimbabwe faced an acute food crisis as a direct result of these policies.

The realisation of failing to control the black people of Rhodesia to fight against the Rhodesian forces led them to the introduction of calling-up of black people secondary qualified students after finishing their secondary school. They were trained in artillery, air forces. They were deployed to fight against their fellow brothers in the bush fighting for the liberation of the black majority rule. It was very unsuccessful. It failed to materialise due to the realisation of whom they were fighting and for what reason. For those who voluntarily joined the Rhodesian forces and were married they had very attractive incentives. The families were well looked after whilst their husbands were in the bush fighting the war. It did not go on for a long time until they had to let go the young men who did not go to join the forces voluntarily. However, most of those who were permanently employed as the Rhodesian forces stayed on; there were many of the Rhodesian forces who were also killed during this war.

* References
Richard Carver and David Sanders, "Why Soames will have to speed food to war zones," *Sunday Times*, London, 23 December 1979

RHODESIAN PERIOD

MY LIFE TIME REVELATIONS

Now let me introduce you to my life revelations. I have always been a woman of adventure always willing to learn. Nothing could stop me doing anything when I put my mind to it. I loved music from an early age I use to have my own song book, which I use to write songs on the charts word for word and sing along, when it was being played on the radio. In my family I can say we were very good in school and we were talented as well. All of us grew up to be professionals in whatever profession we choose.

How we came up to be selling vegetables was due to my mother, who realised that my father's wages were not enough to fully support the family and the extended family as well. Although for my father, it was more of an embarrassment, because people (the society) were seeing him as incapable of not being able to look after his family. My father resorted to buying everything needed in the house. Behind my father's, my mother was looking for money to start her business of selling fruits or vegetables. My mother could not take money from my father's wages because the household expenses were not going to meet the household expenses. On this occasion, she was given 50 shillings by one of my father's nephew, to help her with the household expenses. It was a Saturday afternoon, then she travelled to the vegetable farmer's market to buy a pocket of oranges, which consisted of thirty to forty oranges, she put them in a large bowl priced them according to size. The following day we attended a church service, of which she was in a hurry to give us lunch then go to sell her oranges near the football stadium, to passers-by to and from the football stadium Harare, Zimbabwe. She managed to get a profit that amounted to 100% of the money she used to buy the oranges. When she returned she informed our father who was against the selling business. She persuaded the whole family on carrying on with her business although my father was a bit apprehensive, since my father was a man who understood and realised that, what my mother was doing was helping the family to meet its financial needs. My father still provided with money for groceries every weekend to buy the basic commodities, e.g. meat and ground maize meal, jade bathing soap and marmalade jam his favourite, for his sandwiches, as a child I hated marmalade jam, but now it is one of my favourite. He sometimes uses to ask my mum if she can have a week-end off so that she can be with the family. My mum agreed, on the condition that she would open her stall on Saturday morning only, and then close the whole day Sunday.

My mother believed in women's liberalisation, which was more of an up rise of black women. They formed local women's club, they wanted to better themselves, their families' lives they were against women oppression. They knew that they needed to work very hard in order to raise their families' financial status. My mother and other women realised the need to expand their businesses. They also opened the door to Lever Brothers, Olivine, Nestle, Dairy marketing board, these companies that produced washing and bathing soap, vegetable oil, vegetable margarine, flour, milk, maize meal and etc. started advertising, and marketing using these black women's clubs for cooking demonstrations, and how to use the detergents safely, milk was introduced to schools as well. Children were given milk during breaks. I remember that my mother use to pay our school term time money for us.

Some of these women were better educated than others and they started teaching other women sewing, cookery, housekeeping, dressing competitions, childcare, accounting, health and safety and first aid. They also started going back to school they attending night schools as some of them could not read or write. However, the most surprising and amazing thing is they had the concept of how to count money, calculate their profit or sometimes break even. They started reading, writing, buying the newspaper (*Herald*) reading the current news, those who were good at English would translate to their fellow women and discuss current issues. I use to enjoy hearing my mother discussing the current affairs with my father. My father was educated, more than my mother, but my mother was very intelligent when it comes to family planning and organising of the household running, I can say she could multi task things.

As their ventures expanded, the women realised that they needed bigger premises to sale their vegetables and African cultural products. Within the society if there was anything that, they did not agree with they would demonstrate peacefully, their grievances were solved because the Rhodesian government realised that the majority of the society consisted of women. They demonstrated for anything that was politically incorrect and they usually were resolved, by having a meeting with the government officials. They fought for the 06:00pm to 06:00am curfew to be removed and the Rhodesian government responded immediately and it was removed. They decided to approach their Local Council to give them land and assist them in building market places near all the local Shopping Centres in every black community township. They started going around other black townships to mobilise and encourage other women to join in the liberalisation of women to be allowed to work, and participate in politics and share information about what was going on in the country. They also requested that the municipality should first build vegetable markets instead of a beer garden which the council use to build first near the Shopping centres. Highfield, Mbare, Mufakose, Mabvuku and Tafara were very busy especially over the weekends, which was accessible to many black people from other townships or from rural areas. Bus stations were also built closer to the beer garden, the women never liked it, because, their husbands would come from work they would go straight into the beer garden and come home drunk.

Firstly, the council built some temporary shelters and the women provided their own tables to display their products, e.g. vegetables, traditional foods, traditional wares, such as clay pots, wooden spoons, handmade doormats, summer sunhats, tie-and-dye materials, T/shirts, snuffs and other traditional goods.

After a few meetings with the women the city council agreed to build a proper vegetables and dry African products including cooked African products like boiled fresh peanuts and round nuts. The new market place was built with bricks and mortar. The surfaces were concrete and smooth, underneath there were storage spaces and a lockup door made of steel. The lock up underneath the market space was very vulnerable to thieves; they use to steal left over vegetables. The women and their fellow shop owners agreed that, they put their left over vegetables in the shops storage for free since shops were secure and alarmed or had a security guard. Numbered spaces were allocated to the women who joined were put on waiting list, and then were allocated to them as others retired or move to other areas. They also built toilets, which were for the market people and their customers. Council employees were allocated to clean the surrounding areas of the market and the toilets. The council registered all the traders and collected weekly rentals.

They also decided to expand the whole shopping complex they offered land to black people on which to build more shops. The centre of the market was allocated for those who sold live chickens and eggs. The other side was allocated for those who sold second hand clothes and second hand furniture. Black people built convenient stores, service stations, hairdressers' shops, chemists and hardware shops. Amongst these businesses which were built by emerging African businesspersons and women. There was a little barber shop, which Mr Joshua Nkomo was a frequenter to have his hair cut quite regularly. He never drove to the shopping centre he used to walk. I personally met him there as a young girl and am still very proud to have known him. He had this aroma, when you see him you felt you have seen a leader, he was a very humble man. Very soft spoken this man was a leader and I think he was the chosen few for our country. I always wonder if given the chance how he might have changed our country, Zimbabwe.

Open-air music by emerging African musicians was held every Saturday afternoon at an open space near the market. The township grew very fast. Moreover, we could see tourists from Europe visiting our shops to buy souvenirs to take home, carved stones, walking sticks, snuff, and flower pots made out of wood and clay pots as well, tie and dye materials and tee shirts, and African beads.

We witnessed the first fish and chip shop at the shopping centre, which was opened by an African family. Before this, we had never eaten fish and chips! We used to either roast our potatoes on an open fire or just boil them. It was as if a McDonald's shop opened for the first time in a remote African village! My eldest sister got a job in the fish and chip shop as a cashier. I used to wait for her when she finished work so I could share the leftover fish and chips that her manager would give her.

As for Africans, Sunday's were always for worshipping, most families use to go to church, other families went to dance their traditional dances, others preferred to go separate ways during week-ends whilst some men preferred to go to the beer garden. It was a society that almost had it all, besides all the hardships of segregation and discrimination. My mother is a Christian and a very serious businesswomen she taught us how she was making some profit from her fruit and vegetable sales. She used to order her vegetables from a wholesale market at the main Harare fresh vegetable market (now called Mbare). She used to teach us some marketing techniques how to display the fruits and vegetables to attract customers and customer care in general. Her policy was never to argue with customers, as the customer was always right. I learnt that a seller's aim should be to sell their goods as fast as possible so as to make a quick profit and also to sell the produce while it is still fresh. When customers were satisfied, they will always come back for more. My mother also used to offer credit to some of her customers after gaining trust in them. They in turn would introduce more customers to her. My mother had a very good marketing strategy and good customer relationship with her regular customers. We used to have a credit book for our customers, which allowed us to practice our accounting studies. Customers used to pay at the end of the month or weekly.

The health and food standards department of Rhodesia in the Salisbury city council used to carry out unannounced inspections at the market stalls so it was very important to maintain high standards of hygiene and cleanliness. Inspectors would also check the fruits and vegetables for freshness. These were carried out to ensure that customers were buying uncontaminated food. Food and hygiene was also taught to the vegetable market women by the city council. Women organisations from overseas used to come and carryout conferences with these women and share family ideas.

My mother and her partners who formed the fruit and vegetable market businesses were very hard working women of that time and era. Most of these black women were the first to break the chain of freedom and at the same time managed to afford to pay for their children's education up to university and college level, since it was prestigious. Most of their children went on to pursue successful careers in many fields; some became doctors, nurses, lawyers, accountants, bankers, teachers and other professions. Some managed to pay their children to go and study overseas in countries like Britain and America. Some women managed to help their husbands extend their houses, paid for electricity to be installed in their houses. Others managed to buy houses for their children; some supported their children getting mortgage deposits for their houses. Some managed to buy electrical gadgets like fridges, stoves, televisions and big stereos that were considered luxuries in those days. People, like my family used to throw parties at Christmas as a way of showing off their wealth they would invite all their neighbours. They would provide food and drinks. My mother use to dress us in expensive clothes for all to see. Just as well, the women also followed the fashion trend of the season. Over the weekend one of the pastimes was going to the horse race courses. Borrowdale was the place to be, besides having our own black designated areas, that never bothered us because we knew that those who were there, were from well to do families. They did bet as a syndicate or as individuals, my mother and her now close friends, from the market.

By then our father was in a position to afford to support extended family members who would come and stay with us every now and then. In the African culture families are very closely knit and it is considered as an insult to ask a visiting relative how long they are going to stay. My brothers, sisters and I had to put up with sleeping on the floor at times in order to accommodate respected visiting elderly relatives. Our father had changed his attitude about my mother carrying out her business and he was very supportive. My brothers, sisters, and I used to help our mother at the market after school and over the weekends. At first, we thought our parents were abusing us by making us work so hard but, especially Saturday afternoon when my mum had to go home to be with my father and my other siblings. We as children decided to make a week-end rota so that we can have a week – end off and be home or go out with our friends. I think this hard work paid off as it gave us a good foundation for our lives. It has taught me that when one is climbing up a ladder, one needs to remember every step that one takes so that when you fall you can hold on to one of the steps, pick yourself up and then carry on from there.

I suppose one can understand my background better. I learnt to work hard from a very early age and it is now paying off. At the age of nine, my mother used to give me a buying and selling lesson. She would put money on the table including some of the vegetables and fruits from her stall, and she would play the customer, and I will be the seller. The conversation and the interaction of buying and selling was very interesting to me, she would buy and give me money, and ask me to give her change. If I had done the lesson well that means I had earned myself extra pocket money. This was a life time development lesson; it taught me how to relate to people and how to work with other people.

During the week most of the mother's used to go home around five in the afternoon, we would have returned from school around three-thirty in the afternoon, then go home to change our school uniforms have a snack then go to the market to sell the left over produce. Equipped with the knowledge that we had learned from our mothers, we would try to sell the vegetable so that when we go home with a lot of money our mother will be very grateful and that means a lot of pocket money. We use to call customers and tell them that we have a lot to offer and other products are now free, which was a true but we will have calculated to break even or make a small profit.

On one occasion in the evening I mistook one man who was already buying from our neighbour's stall for my uncle the man quickly apologised to the stallholder and came to us and bought most of our left over vegetables. This man was not our uncle, but I think he felt guilty as I called him 'uncle'. My sister and I had to help him carry what he had bought to his car. My sister did not say anything she could not look me in the eyes because the other woman was so furious, standing in akimbo in disbelief to what had just happened she just watched in shock. We finished parking the few goods left. We did not even say bye to her we ran home, as soon as we opened the gate we burst into laughter that my mother was thinking we had run away from the police officer because maybe we did not close the stall in time. The stall used to be closed at 19:00hrs if you extend the time you would be arrested and pay a fine. Sometimes as children we would run away if they ask us to go with them to the police station, because they will be people still walking around then we would just hide behind someone, then run home. We asked our mother to count the money we had, and she wondered how we had so much, we told her what had happened and the whole family burst into laughter. The following day the lady the owner of the next stall told our mother what had happened, our mother apologised.

In a way, our mother was trying to tell her to leave her children alone to let them enjoy the stall and the experience. She used to be on her stall from morning until closing down time. Each time we think of that incident with my sister, we still laugh, and all I can say is, "Oh! Gone are the days when we enjoyed life in Rhodesia". We used to enjoy going to assist our mother at the vegetable stall, because she used to spoil us with money to the hairdresser's and to the musical festivals which were occasionally held in the nearby stadium. We did attended all of them, all the musicians who visited our country, Percy Sledge, The Hurricanes, Miriam Makeba, Ladysmith Black Mambazo, from South Africa, and other famous Zimbabwean musicians, Thomas Mapfumo, Oliver Mtukudzi.

Life was just good for us we used to go shopping with my father for our clothes and school uniforms. We had a very strong bond amongst our parents and ourselves. These market place vegetable salespersons broke the chain of freedom of women, "some call it women liberalisation" they were allowed to work, participate in politics and in any society problems they were living in. They became the voice of black women. During that time, we had enough money to live on. These women managed to help their husbands to buy the title deeds for their houses, helped extended their houses to give a good comfort to their families. We saw the introduction of electricity in their houses. Telephone lines were there for their communication purposes, business meeting and to communicate with their sons and daughters now staying away from home, or have travelled to study in Europe. Talk of televisions and Supersonic radios, it was now more of a competition than a luxury, as to what do you have in your household. The luxury started to flow. Electrical appliances were now a necessity for the home.

Houses became homes, we were never disadvantaged as such, we went to school, fees were paid and we used to enjoy all the African tale stories, jokes that our father used to share with us. We now respect that our mother was very focused about our future. As the townships were now growing into small towns and becoming popular, we saw the building of proper recreation centres, football stadiums started cropping up as well. Bandits, serving times for the crime, were sentenced to work in the development of the townships. They built the recreation centres, football stadiums, council beer gardens and sewage pipes. The council beer garden, which sold the African brewed beer, hob brewed beer.

The set-up of having a bus station, a stadium and a beer garden situated at the same proximity used to annoy many housewives. People used to get paid weekly. Some housewives used to stand by the bus stop or by the beer garden gates to get some pay monies out of their husbands before they spend all of their wages on beer. It was interesting to watch some women pulling their husbands out of the beer garden. Some of the situations were quite embarrassing others were dramatic when the wives snatch off the pay envelopes from their husbands. We had it all it was a society which was full of humour and serious business at the same time. Other women from the vegetable stalls decided to try their luck on cooked street foods, like fried fresh chicken pieces, caterpillars with chilli spiced sauces or just spiced with curry powder and chillies. Other delicacies were boiled pigs, cows and chicken offal's. They were doing very well in selling street food. But the municipality refused to build shelters for them, since the council sold snacks within the beer garden.

As far as school was concerned according to the Rhodesian Government, every child had a right to go to school. Truancy was a crime. Parent had to send their children to school, and pay school fees. That was one good thing about the Rhodesian Government. The teachers were very dedicated to give the right education and prepare their pupils for a brighter future. The teachers were respected by society and their pupils respected them as well. The thing is during the Rhodesian period educated people reaped the fruits of the seeds that they sowed. Going to school was a must in my family.

My primary school education was full of fun and adventure. Firstly, I went to the same primary school as my eldest brother. My mother and father thought it was a good idea, because he would watch me and also walk with me to and from school. He used to take me straight into my class, during breaks he used to come to check on me. I liked going to school during the first term. The second term of my first year in school, I completely changed; I did not like school, because of our teacher. She slapped me, because I failed to add numbers on board. My peers also failed to answer but they were not slapped. I went home and told my mother. The following day my mother came with me to school and asked if it was true that she slapped me, the teacher told my mum that it was true and it will not happen again. I was never slapped again, and I was happy. At the end of the year, we did a school play, which the parents were invited. Our teacher taught us a song about oranges and how good and nutritious they were. My mother, with excitement brought me two big and beautiful oranges from her market stall. The day of the play, we went to school as usual. The play was to be held in the school hall. We sat on the floor and practiced. The session was delayed, and as children, we three quarters of the group, we ate our oranges, which were meant for holding and showing the crowds and parents. My father and mother and the crowd laughed. We managed to carry on singing, and we were lifting our hands empty. My elder sister and elder brothers used to help us with our homework. Our father was very good at story telling before bed.

The following year, my young sister started school, so my mother decided to transfer me to join her on the same school. That is how I was moved from my first school. My mother had our young brother when my young sister was considered to be the last born. She was so attached to mum she still wanted to sit on our mother's lap when she had our young brother who is the last born. When he started school we were all so excited to see how he was going to do in school, this is the guy who had mum's milk until he was almost four years old. He stopped sucking milk from our mother because of my elder brothers laughing at him and stopping taking him out to play. It used to be funny, because when he was thirst he use to ask mum to sit down to have milk, and he never liked drinking water.

My young brother was extremely intelligent. He was good in science subjects and he went to college and studied mechanical engineering. He was not into sports. I liked running and swimming. Both my elder brothers and sister were very good swimmers and they competed in school competitions. Myself and my young sister only learned how to swim and were just good swimmers with our peers. My eldest brother was competing in the national high school competitions. We won a number of trophies. My other elder brother was very good in school and used to get excellent results every year. We were all good in school, when we completed primary school and started attending secondary schools. That is when everyone was now showing what they were good at. Secondary school that is when we had a teacher for each subject it was a new experience and having home work in each and every subject. My brother's, my elder sister and young sister excelled in mathematics. I can say I was good, but not as good as them three, especially our elder sister who was good at algebra. I was very good at History, geography, accounting and economics. I grew up not very health, I was always ill, with stomach cramps or headaches. I was very thin people thought that I was not part of the family because everyone was health and fit.

After secondary school, we all started looking for places at colleges and universities. My eldest brother started studying salesmanship, which our father encouraged him to do. My father organised a job for him in his company where he was offered a job. He was still studied very hard whilst working at our fathers company. When he finished his studies, the company was in the process of opening outlets throughout the country. He was assigned to design the shop floor and make flyers. He was quickly promoted to a product promotion manager. This promotion came with a package that included company car, company house and other benefits that included part of his children fees being paid by the company. My other brother was into purchasing and supplying of which he studied up to a master's degree. My elder sister was a private secretary. She did typing and Pitman's short-hand. My young sister went to college and did a teacher's training diploma for four years. She completed, got married and was teaching her favourite subject mathematics to students from year nine to general certificate of education. As for me, I worked as a shop assistant whilst I was also looking for other jobs. I was informed by one of our family friend that the public service commission was recruiting clerks and registry clerks to work in the ministry offices. I took a day off from my job I went to the public services commission offices recruitment centre. As I walked in I was very nervous, but the receptionist told me not to worry. I was given a form and a pen that she asked me to fill in and come with it the following day for an interview. I phoned my manager where I was working as a sales lady and asked for another day off, she agreed that I could go for the interview for a better job and if it did not work, I was welcome to go back. I did not sleep with the excitement I even failed to eat and I had butterflies in my stomach. These jobs were only for whites and coloured people, but the doors had opened us, we had the qualifications to join the civil service. I attended my interview at ten o'clock the following day. I felt a bit low and felt that I had no hope as there were so many of us applying we had to write a test in English and a bit of mathematics.

After the test we were seated in the waiting room. They urgently needed staff by the look of it so we were given our test results and told who got the job after just two hours! They provided us with drinks tea, coffee and soft drinks, but nobody drank because it was nerve racking. The door opened, the interviewers came in with a list and told us who had a job, and my name was called. I became numb from my head down to my toes. She said congratulations you got the job I only managed to say thank you. I was told that I was going to be a registry clerk in the ministry, and to report for work on Monday at 8am. When I got home my mother asked me how it went I could not talk she asked me if I wanted something to eat I managed to just say no! Went to bed and cried tears of joy in disbelief because this was an out of reach job during those days.

I spent the whole day in my room until my father came back from work. He asked how it went; my mother said she didn't know. My father called me he thinking that I didn't get the job. He started comforting me and reassuring me that it was not the end of the world it's only the beginning I should try next time since they were giving people an opportunity to try again. I told my father that I got the job. In disbelief he laughed with joy and asked me why I was looking so miserable. I told him that I did not expect to get the job. He offered me some money to go and buy good clothes for an office job. My eldest brothers gave me money too to buy myself underclothes as they stated it. That weekend was full of joy, happiness, and celebration.

I started working as a registry clerk. My workmates were a mixture of all colours of all people. Moreover, the head of the registry was an Indian woman who was very nice. She was the one who carried out the training for newly recruited staff and all the in-house training for registry clerks. After a week I was offered my own desk and codex machine which I used for filing letters in alphabetic order. I enjoyed getting up every morning and catching a bus to work. Just being in the city centre working made me felt classy and educated. I started following my passion for fashion. I dressed well and followed every fashion trend during those days. Platform shoes, bellbottoms, afro wigs, and knee-high stockings I wore them all. I even wore stilettos. I even tried my luck at a modelling agency, but my height let me down.

As time progressed, banks followed suit and started recruiting blacks as bank tellers and clerks. I had gained confidence in myself by now and I was on the move again, for a well-paid job. I started with a building society because the commercial banks had not opened up yet. I joined the Central African Building Society. The salary was good and had all the luxuries that I wanted. I worked as a clerk in the client's queries department, and at the reception sometimes. I used to update clients' passbook as they were called in those days, enter their interest. I decided to join the commercial banks. I got a job as a relief bank teller, covering shifts for staff that were on holiday or ill where our bank had a bank. I would work for as long as I was needed. Some of the relief shifts lasted up to three weeks or more. That forced me travel and see the country's big and small towns. I had an out of town allowance and I stayed in five star hotels with all meals, and had dry cleaners allowance. I had the time of my life. After a few years working in the bank, our parents retired. My eldest sister took over our mother's vegetable market stall she was also doing very well as a single mother of two. After a few years working in the bank, our parents retired. My eldest sister took over our mother's vegetable market stall she was also doing very well as a single mother of two. My brothers were doing very well in their jobs. I and my sister were also doing well in our jobs.

Following my adventures and wanting to learn landed me in Eastern Europe. What an adventure, as far as education was considered during those years back then, it was the key to success. Talking about getting out of the country to go and study in Europe or any country outside Zimbabwe was for those who could afford sending their children to learn abroad, or those who would have excelled in their studies and have applied for sponsorship through the British Council. It was very prestigious. In a way it showed that the student is genius and can go and pursue their studies in England or in Europe.

After receiving our independence, the United Nations offered scholarship support to people of Zimbabwe to go and study abroad. Firstly these opportunities were granted to the ex-combatants to go and study in their chosen fields, which were specifically selected for the development of our country after the war. These courses consisted of fields in medicine, veterinary, zoology, chemical engineering, agronomy, agricultural economics, economics, media communications, computer programmers and etc.

As times goes on it was opened for all the school leavers who had good secondary school grades and were willing to study abroad. The scholarships were advertised in the Herald Newspaper for people to apply and go through the interviewing process. The selection committee selected students following their grades in GCE 'O' Levels and 'A' Levels. They also requested students to write a short summary on areas of study they were interested in. Countries to go and study were mostly in the Eastern Europe, Russia, Bulgaria, Greece, Romania, and German and in South America especially Cuba for those who were interested in science subjects.

STUDYING ABROAD

I submitted my application to study abroad. I had an open mind about it. I did not know whether my application was going to be successful or not. It came as a shock when I received a letter to attend an interview by the selection committee and was asked to submit my certificates and passport size photos including my passport. I was still not sure that I was going to be successful. After waiting for a week, I received a call, I was asked to report to the scholarship office where I was informed that my application was successful and I was going to study abroad. The news was so overwhelming, that I did shed a tear. The team congratulated me and gave me my passport which had been stamped a visa in it and a one way ticket to Europe.

    I returned to work, where I was a working as a bank-teller and worked as usual. I did not want anyone to know about my leaving the country, for Europe. I informed my immediate manager at the bank, who congratulated me and managed to keep it a secret. I went home after work and managed to keep my secret. After work on Saturday, I went travel bag shopping by myself. I bought a set of suitcases. When I returned home with my shopping, I decided to announce my secret, whilst the whole family was there. Everybody was shocked, due to the fact that I had a serious relationship with a guy that they thought I was going to marry that year. In my eyes I did not see any bright future with this guy. I assessed the situation and realised that the relationship was not good for me. I still wanted to go to university and further my studies, but for him working in an office as a wages clerk was enough for him. I did not want to break my family's hearts by telling them that I was done with this guy. I wanted to be a successful person and work as a professional. He thought that I was joking when I broke the news to him I was leaving the country to go and study abroad. He laughed his lungs out. When the day for my departure finally arrived and I was going, that is when it kicked in that I was leaving and for over seven years. I saw him crying, I told him that I have given him time and space to reflect his life and future. My whole family and friends came to see me off to Europe. I was sad, to leave my family, but happy to go and study a new much promising profession. I promised myself that I was going to be strong for me and my family. I have always wanted to be a person with a profession. I achieved my goal with flying colours and I became a graduate.

BOOK 3

ZIMBABWEAN PERIOD

ZIMBABWE INDEPENDENCE

In 1974, while still incarcerated, Mugabe was elected – with the powerful influence of Edgar Tekere – to take over the reins of ZANU after a no-confidence vote was passed on Ndabaningi Sithole – Mugabe himself abstained from voting. His time in prison burnished his reputation and helped his cause. Following a South African détente initiative, Mugabe was released from prison in December 1974 along with other Nationalist leaders and having initially travelled to Zambia, where he was ignored by Kenneth Kaunda, returned then left once again in April 1975 for Mozambique assisted by a Dominican nun, where he was later placed in temporary protective custody by President Samora Machel. According to Eddie Cross who participated in interviews of the leadership at that time to determine their views on the "longer term future", Mugabe's political viewpoint was that "a new 'progressive' society could not be constructed on the foundations of the past (and) that they would have to destroy most of what had been built up after 1900 before a new society, based on subsistence and peasant values could be constructed".

Mugabe unilaterally assumed control of ZANU after the death of Herbert Chitepo on 18 March 1975. Later that year, after squabbling with Ndabaningi Sithole, Mugabe formed a militant ZANU faction, leaving Sithole to lead the moderate Zanu (Ndonga) party. Many opposition leaders mysteriously died during this time (Including one who allegedly died in a car crash, although the car was rumoured to have been riddled with bullet holes at the scene of the accident). Additionally, an opposing newspaper's printing press was bombed and its journalists tortured.

AGREEMENT LANCASTER HOUSE: 1979-1980

Under pressure from Henry Kissinger, Prime Minister of South Africa B. J. Vorster persuaded Ian Smith, the sitting prime minister at the time, to accept in principle that white minority rule could not continue indefinitely. On 3 March 1978 Bishop Abel Muzorewa, Ndabaningi Sithole and other moderate leaders signed an agreement at the Governor's Lodge in Salisbury, which paved the way for an interim power-sharing government, in preparation for elections. The elections were won by the United African National Council under Bishop Abel Muzorewa, but international recognition did not follow and sanctions were not lifted. The two 'Patriotic Front' groups under Mugabe and Joshua Nkomo refused to participate and continued the war.

The incoming government did accept an invitation to talks at Lancaster House in September 1979. A ceasefire was negotiated for the talks, which were attended by Smith, Mugabe, Nkomo, Zvobgo and others. Eventually the parties to the talks agreed on a new constitution for a new Republic of Zimbabwe with elections in February 1980. The Lancaster Agreement saw Mugabe make two important and contentious concessions. First, he allowed 20 seats to be reserved for whites in the new Parliament, and second, he agreed to a ten-year moratorium on constitutional amendments. His return to Zimbabwe in December 1979, following the completion of the Lancaster House Agreement, was greeted with enormous supportive crowds. After a campaign marked by intimidation from all sides, mistrust from security forces and reports of full ballot boxes found on the road, the Shona majority was decisive in electing Mugabe to head the first government as prime minister on 4 March 1980. ZANU won 57 out of 80 Common Roll seats in the new parliament, with the 20 white seats all going to the Rhodesian Front.

Mugabe, whose political support came from his Shona-speaking homeland in the north, attempted to build Zimbabwe on a basis of an uneasy coalition with his ZAPU rivals, whose support came from the Ndebele-speaking south, and with the white minority. Mugabe sought to incorporate ZAPU into his ZANU led government and ZAPU's military wing into the army. ZAPU's leader, Joshua Nkomo, was given a series of cabinet positions in Mugabe's government. However, Mugabe was torn between this objective and pressures to meet the expectations of his own ZANU followers for a faster pace of social change.

In 1983, Mugabe fired Nkomo from his cabinet, triggering bitter fighting between ZAPU supporters in the Ndebele-speaking region of the country and the ruling ZANU. Mugabe accused the Ndebele tribe of plotting to overthrow him after sacking Nkomo. Between 1982 and 1985, the military crushed armed resistance from Ndebele groups in the provinces of Matabeleland and the Midlands, leaving Mugabe's rule secure. Mugabe has been accused by the BBC's Panorama programme of committing mass murder during this period of his rule, after the show investigated claims made by political activist Gary Jones that Mugabe had been instrumental in removing him and his family from his farmland. A peace accord was negotiated in 1987. ZAPU merged into the Zimbabwe African National Union-Patriotic Front (ZANU-PF) on 22 December 1988. Mugabe brought Nkomo into the government once again as a vice-president.

ZIMBABWEAN PERIOD

GETTING OUR INDEPENDENCE IN 1980

Getting our independence in 1980, was it a dream that came true! I always wonder was this genuine or it was a mockery. when I look back and reflect to what the people of Zimbabwe were promised, for example; free education, and free medical services for all just to mention a few. This has been an everyday thought. The way I experienced the Independence years; it brought instability, political and economic failure, that's my opinion. The country went downhill financially; the Zimbabwean dollar lost its value, until it was removed from the international market. People migrated to neighbouring countries and other countries abroad. Some like me travelled abroad. In my research I came across a lot of information that I have incorporated in my book. Some of it sensitive and some of it breaks my heart, as the following information.

BILL BERKELEY, 1989

The sense of hope and optimism that accompanied the birth of Zimbabwe as an independent state in 1980 survived for several years. In keeping with his promises about reconciliation, Robert Mugabe strove to build a good working relationship with his former white adversaries. He appointed two white ministers to his cabinet and retained the services of the former Rhodesian armed forces commander, General Peter Walls, as the country's military chief. He even kept in place the head of intelligence, Ken Flower, who had previously spent considerable effort trying to organise Mugabe's assassination. At one of their first meetings in Mugabe's office, Flower was anxious to explain about the various attempts that the Rhodesians had made to kill him because, regardless of their crimes, the Rhodesian officials had to stay, because of the well-being of the security apparatus depended on it. The other reason for extending an olive branch to Rhodesian security officials was political. Mugabe was eager to avoid antagonizing the economically crucial white community. Although many whites migrated soon after independence, the farming community has generally stayed and benefited from an agricultural boom, whilst whites occupied many important positions in commerce and business.

All appointed ministers, the government and government servants were indemnified under Rhodesian law for acts carried out in good faith in defence of national security. However, there was no indication that the Zimbabwean government ever considered the possibility of nullifying the indemnity legislation in order to prosecute the human rights violators. In these circumstances, the Zimbabwean government decided that reconciliation rather than prosecution best served the interests of national stability.

Berkeley further comments: "Some Zimbabweans cite that record as precedent for sweeping the more recent conflict under the rug."

Sheepishly, after independence we never understood what was in store for us. The old system was still running in parallel with the new system. We had the Rhodesian government security adopted system through and through. There still was a lot of intimidation in the air. People were still harassed or even killed without being sentenced properly, and justice was never met.

As an observer from afar, life in Zimbabwe was good for others, whilst others were suffering the atrocities of war, which was still going on in Matebeleland. At the back of my mind I understood that the human rights of people were violated and never repaired. People disappeared and people were killed but the perpetrators were never brought forward to courts and charged for the atrocities they caused. When it comes to tribalism, Zimbabweans do not have hard feelings for other tribes.

There are quite a number of issues that were mentioned. Nevertheless, people as usual they talked amongst themselves, even grieved amongst them. There was never support from the government. The only people who were worried about the people's welfare were the council of churches of Zimbabwe and The Amnesty International, which was usually never taken serious when they reported of human rights violation, especially on prisoners.

The electoral support for ZANU-PF and ZAPU in the 1980 election largely followed ethnic lines. With the understanding of the Rhodesian information that I have equipped myself with, it seems that the Lobengula issue, of the Rudd Concession, and the fact that the Ndebele people were killing the Mashona speaking people still lingers in the air of everything that they do in the country. As much as the people of Zimbabwe do not open up to talk about it, but the division has been there. All ZAPU's 20 seats came from Matabeleland where the predominant ethnic group is the Ndebele, or from the ethnically mixed Midlands. ZANU-PF won no seats in Matebeland and drew most of its support from the majority Shona speakers. The original split between ZANU and ZAPU in the 1960s had nothing to do with the Ndebele-Shona division but a combination of political accident and conscious tribalism by some party leaders combined to make it a potent factor by the time of independence.

The conflict first blew up in the army. At independence, it was agreed to integrate the ZANLA and ZIPRA** guerrillas into a single national army alongside with the former Rhodesian forces. If anything, the former guerrillas were probably less prone to party or ethnic sectarianism than some of their political leaders. However, there was a widespread perception that the fighters who had made the greatest sacrifices for Zimbabwe's independence were having the least share benefits. Such frustration erupted into fighting between former ZANLA and ZIPRA guerrillas encamped at Entumbane Township in Bulawayo awaiting integration. Initial fighting in November 1980 died down after a few days.

* Lawyers Committee, op cit., p90-1
** The Zimbabwe African National Liberation Army (ZANLA) was the military wing of ZANU; the Zimbabwe People's Liberation Army (ZIPRA) was its ZAPU counterpart.

A second outburst in February 1981 spread to other groups of guerrillas awaiting integration and was only ended when the government deployed ex-Rhodesians units and their air force against former ZIPRA personnel, killing more than 100. This action prompted many ex-ZIPRA members to desert and go back to the bush with their guns. These desertions accelerated a year later when the government announced that it had uncovered arms caches on ZAPU-owned properties. Joshua Nkomo and the other ZAPU Ministers were sacked from the government and former ZIPRA leaders, notably Dumiso Dabengwa and Lookout Musuku, the deputy army commander, were arrested and charged with treason. They were later acquitted, but rearrested and detained without charge until 1986.* From early 1982 a military Task Force led by Lieutenant-Colonel Lionel Dyke, a former Rhodesian officer, was deployed in Matebeleland North against the ex-ZIPRA "dissidents," as the government called them. There were frequent reports of detention and torture of villagers. One eyewitness from Tsholotsho is reported as describing what happened when the Task force came to the village:

The soldiers beat and hit us and threatened us in a terrible way. They accused us of feeding dissidents. They hit one old woman and said that she was a mother of dissidents. Then the white soldier picked one boy and asked him what he was going to say. He said he knew nothing to say about dissidents. The white soldier took his gun from his belt and just shot the boy in the head. Just in front of us.*

In January 1983, the Task force was replaced by the Fifth Brigade, a unit which had been specially trained by North Korean military advisers and which was outside the normal command structure of the army, being directly under the control of the

Prime Minister's office. The Brigade appeared to be almost exclusively composed of Shona-speaking ex-ZANLA combatants. In the weeks followed, the Fifth Brigade carried out many killings of villagers in Matebeleland North. Reports indicated that often they visited villages with lists of ZAPU officials and sympathisers, who were singled out and killed.

They made little attempt to engage the "dissidents" militarily. There was an ugly strand of tribalism in the behaviour of the Fifth Brigade: the Ndebele were being punished for crimes their ancestors were supposed to have committed against the Shona. Finally, in mid-1993, Mugabe responded to international pressure and withdrew the Fifth Brigade from Matebeland. A commission of inquiry was set up to investigate allegations of army abuses; although it submitted a report to the government, its findings were never made public.

However, at the beginning of 1984, the Fifth Brigade was redeployed in Matebeleland South and the pattern of abuse was repeated. Again, there were reports of army killings and torture at a number of ad hoc army camps: Belaghwe, Sun Yet Sen and Mphoengs. However, this time there was also a strict dusk to dawn curfew and restrictions on the movement of food into the area. This was the height of a severe drought, which affected the whole of Zimbabwe, but Matebeleland South worst of all. There had been some attempt to restrict food supplies in Matebeleland North in 1983 but now Operation Turkey was being wholeheartedly revived. Again, there was an international outcry and the Fifth Brigade was withdrawn. The journalist who played the greatest role in exposing the killings, Peter Godwin of the London Sunday Times, was expelled from the country. (Nick Worrall of The Guardian had been expelled the previous year.)

Exactly how many people died at the hands of the Fifth Brigade will never be known. The Justice and Peace Commission stated in 1983 that it had gathered firm evidence of 469 civilian killings "for the most part by government soldiers." Clearly, the actual death toll was much higher – 1500 would be a conservative estimate.

A tiny handful of cases were security force members brought to justice for these killings. In June 1988, the four soldiers were among the 75 members of the security forces released under the amnesty.*

The initial "dissidents" were from the left wing of ZIPRA and had historically maintained strong links with the African National Congress of South Africa (ANC). Nevertheless, the South African government saw the instability in Matebeleland as a chance to pursue its own ends by arming and sponsoring its own "dissidents" bands. While the security forces were carrying out their abuses, the "dissidents" were committing their own atrocities against the civilian population and, on occasions, against others such as tourists and missionaries. One of the incidents, which grabbed international attention, occurred in November 1987 when "dissidents" hacked to death 16 members of a Protestant mission at Esigodini, including babies and small children. Such brutality affected the hapless people of Matebeleland for six years or so.

However, in certain instances there is evidence to suggest that killings were carried out by "dissidents" but by "pseudo-gangs" of the security forces. The tactics of impersonating guerrillas while committing atrocities was used by the Rhodesian forces in the independence war. In November 1985 Luke and Jean Khumalo, a Methodist headmaster and his wife, were killed at Thekwane School in Matebeleland South. The official version was that the dissidents were responsible. However, there were a number of unanswered questions.

Why did soldiers at an army camp three kilometres away not intervene, when the attackers were at the school for several hours, firing shots and burning buildings? The army did not even arrive when the school staff sent for help after the attackers had left. Why were the attackers wearing military uniform? In addition, why did they leave a note saying that Luke and Jean Khumalo were being killed for passing information to Amnesty International's call for an inquiry into the killings; the government stated that it had captured a member of the "dissident" band responsible. However, as far as Africa Watch can tell, no one has been charged with the murders.

In early 1985, a new pattern of human rights abuse emerged. Dozens possibly hundreds-of people throughout Matebeland and Midlands "disappeared as a result of night time abductions by armed men. The government's explanation was that the "disappeared people had gone to join the "dissidents" but there are a number of factors suggesting that the security forces were in fact responsible. The victims were often middle-aged or old men – not the young men who might be expected to join the "dissidents." They were often driven away in vehicles – yet there are no recorded instances of "dissidents" having vehicles. On occasions, vehicles were identified as belonging to the security forces and sometimes the tracks were followed to the military camps. The armed men who came often spoke only poor Ndebele – the "dissidents" were usually fluent Ndebele speakers.* none of those abducted has reappeared since the "dissidents" were amnestied and came out of the bush in May 1988.

In late 1985, Amnesty International publicly stated its concern over torture in Zimbabwe. It followed this with a memorandum to the government detailing 21 cases of torture and seeking an impartial investigation. A report by the Lawyers Committee for Human Rights in May 1986 provided a more comprehensive review of the human rights situation. As with the expulsion of journalists who reported the Matebeleland killings, the government response was to blame the bearer of bad news. All allegations of torture were categorically denied. Amnesty International, which had adopted many members of the government as "prisoners of conscience" during their long spells in Rhodesian jails, was denounced as an "enemy of Zimbabwe." Former prisoner of conscience Robert Mugabe described it as "Amnesty Lies International," while home affairs Minister Enos Nkala (another Amnesty International alumnus) threatened to detain anyone who provided the organization with information. Is this how people are supposed to be treated after voting for a black majority, what is the difference between the Rhodesian rule of Zimbabwe and Zimbabwe rule? When you look at it its' like a playground of evil people who have created their own experimental ritual research on animals, or even animals deserve better treatment as well. They are not allowed to exercise their human rights, the world is watching, Africa is watching, and so, what is next? Don't you wonder?

Furthermore, the Amnesty International never stopped fighting for human rights mechanism to be put in place but there was always a high huddle to jump for them. The December 1987 unity agreement was followed by a Cabinet reshuffle which brought ZAPU Ministers back into the government for the first time since 1982, but also removed the hard line anti-ZAPU Enos Nkala from the Ministry of Home Affairs and replaced him with Moven Mahachi. Soon after his appointment, Mahachi set about releasing the remaining Emergency Powers detainees. By April 1988 only a handful remained, who were released to mark the eighth anniversary of independence. Also on Independence Day Mugabe announced an amnesty for all those "dissidents" still in the bush who surrendered by the end of May. Some 113 did so and Matabeleland's security problems were largely at an end. Under the terms of the amnesty, none of those who surrendered could be prosecuted for crimes committed while they were in the bush. There was considerable popular discontent when "Gayigusu" – Morgan Sango Nkomo – took advantage of the amnesty. He had been responsible for the November 1987 massacre of the missionaries at Esigodini and other atrocities. Just to mention the least, because some of the other information is very sensitive if you are human enough and very sickening. I never thought in my whole life that some of these things were happening but after reading and talking to a number of people from all over Zimbabwe, I was shocked and felt sick and very disillusioned about the Zimbabwean government.

The other thing that I cannot come to terms with is the violation of rights to the payments of damages. On this Zimbabwe has a poor record. In 1986 Mugabe was questioned in Parliament about the government's failure to pay damages awarded against it unlawful arrest and detention. He replied: If government – and

I want to say this as a matter of principle – were to be awarding damages and paying huge sums of money that are involved in these cases, some of which are of a petty nature, government would in my view be using the taxpayers' money wrongfully. It is true that government has not paid damages. Where, for example, a person suffers injury as a result of an accident involving on the one side, a vehicle driven by a government employee, we have paid-have not refused. However, where people take advantage of liberal situation to go to court and win on technicalities, they should not expect that the government is going to use the people's resources to enrich them when we believe in some cases that they are wrongdoers.*

It had apparently not occurred to the Prime Minister that the misuse of taxpayers' money came with the unlawful arrest, not the subsequent award of damages to the wronged parties. There is no legal remedy in Zimbabwe if the State refuses to pay damages awarded by the court.**

In any case, when one reads some of these issues involving human rights it becomes clear that there was never law laid out for the welfare of the civilians, the people, but the law had to be given in for the perpetrators, or the violators of the human rights. There was a clear indication that the government employees, especially the law enforcement group, soldiers, air force, police force. The people of Zimbabwe were practically exposed and as much as they would like to feel, they had a roof over their heads, but reading and researching has opened up my mind that there was no one to give people of Zimbabwe security that was eminent for them. People of Zimbabwe feared to air their views, stopped their children to say anything that has to do with the government or else they will be maimed or killed or disappear forever. I can see through a wall in my memory that is how they lived, I can imagine even by trying to exercise their rights through the ballot box by voting during the elections times, they will still be maimed or killed. Because they are dealing with people who never had them at heart and treat them with respect, inhumane is the norm.

* Incidentally, the case of Dabengwa and Masuku also illustrates the folly of retaining former Rhodesian CIO officers. The ex-ZIPRA army officers who carried out the catching of arms appear to have a police agent working under the orders of Mart Calloway, the head of CIO in Hwange. Calloway later defected to South Africa where he became a crucial figure in organising support for the "dissidents". The continued detention of the two popular ZIPRA leaders was an important factor provoking anti-government sentiment in Matebeleland. Calloway's role is outlined in Joseph Hanion, "Destabilisation and the Battle to Reduce Dependence" in Colin Stoneman (Ed), Zimbabwe's Prospects, London 1988.

** "Rhodesian troops prop up Mugabe," Africa Now, July 1984

* Article 2 (3) of the International Covenant on Civil and Political Rights

(Which Zimbabwe has not signed or ratified) amplifies the point: Each State Party to the present Covenant undertakes:

a. To ensure that any person whose rights or freedoms are as herein recognized are violated shall have an effective remedy, notwithstanding that the violation has been committed by persons acting in an official capacity;

b. To ensure that any person claiming such remedy shall have his right thereto determined by competent judicial, administrative or legislative authorities, or by any other competent authority provided for by the legal system of the State, and to develop the possibilities of judicial remedy;

c. To ensure that the competent authorities shall enforce such remedies when granted.

* Speech of July 16, 1986, cited in G Feltoe, A Guide to Zimbabwe Cases Relating to Security, Emergency Powers and Unlawful arrest and Detention, Legal Foundation, Harare 1988, pp8.
** Ibid, pp8-9

Although the Justice and Peace Commission continued its work on behalf of detainees and their dependents, as well as bringing the High Court action on behalf of the dependents of "Disappeared" people from Silobela. The commission continues to submit details of its concerns confidentially to government, as well as making public statements on important human rights issues. Despite these occasional problems, the prestige of the Justice and Peace Commission has usually enabled it to carry out its investigations without official harassment.

At that moment, Zimbabwe was now in a position or rather appeared more open to investigations by international human rights organisations. In October 1988 there was a warm official welcome for a "Human Rights Now!" concert sponsored by Amnesty International in Harare and Zimbabwean officials have been ready to respond to Africa Watch's inquiries about detentions and other reported human rights abuses.

Another non-governmental organisation, the Legal Resources Foundation, set up in 1985, has been doing important work in making legal services and knowledge of legal rights accessible to a broader public. This has been achieved through publications, legal advice sessions and training programs. In April 1989, Bulawayo Legal Projects Centre, run by the foundation, began a training program for police and other law enforcement officers in various human rights aspects of criminal procedure.

ZIMBABWEAN PERIOD

START OF DECLINE

When Mugabe came to power he kept one-party system. The government assiduously wooed the white population of around 100,000 because of their significant economic role. During that period a number of white farmers joined ZANU-PF. Mugabe had succeeded in attracting support of long-standing members of Ian Smith's Rhodesian Front notably former Justice Minister Chris Anderson and Charles Duke who both held ministerial posts in the army and security services of Rhodesia. In 1987 the government had a change of heart by introducing an important democratic reform by abolishing the 20% of parliamentary seats reserved exclusive for whites. Although there was no general election at this time, any political party including one with a predominantly white membership was entitled to contest any parliamentary seat.

The never-ending decline of the Zimbabwean economy has been virtually entirely due to government's actions. But its comprehensible ill-conceived basis of attaining much-needed land reform and the near-criminal mismanagement easily showed the failings in its government policies. The government's policies and actions did more to fuel hyperinflation than any other causes. Through the government abuses of international recognised fundamental principles of human rights, justice, law, order and respect for property rights, which were compounded by a continuous barrage of vitriolic insults targeted many of the international countries. The Zimbabwean government vigorously discouraged foreign direct investment and provoked the withholding of the much needed developmental aid and balance of payment support. By the government rigid resistance to extensive privatisation of companies and its unwillingness or inability to fund companies adequately, concurrently with unwillingness to effect meaningful managerial appointments in many of them. The infrastructural support base of the economy collapsed and still collapsing more and more, with inadequate availability of energy, disastrously ineffectual telecommunications and much else retarding economic activity. To any educated person this declining of a country's economy clearly showed that there was no future, no life. People of Zimbabwe started to make certain comparison to the previous life that they knew during the Rhodesian period. It's so sad to hear people saying, under the sun we never suffered like this during the Rhodesian regime. They go to bed not knowing what tomorrow is like. They do not plan for tomorrow.

Obtaining a birth or death certificate was just an hour's job or less. Nowadays it's a whole day's job. Government offices "Wow"! They do not seem to be like the ones we used to go to, the set-up, the atmosphere, with no air conditioners. As much as I do sympathize with people who are working in these government offices their wages are below poverty datum line. They cannot afford to do anything with the wages they receive. By the look of it I cannot imagine how they are managing. So, for their survival they always ask for a bit of extra money from you. It is tactfully done in a way that one does not recognize that you are paying extras for the staff to be able to sustain themselves and their families. It is much more of survival of the fittest.

The black market is the backbone of the Zimbabwean economy. Corruption has risen exponentially. Supermarkets are full of foods, but no one buys. They would rather travel to South Africa and buy their groceries in South African Currency than using US dollars.

Road-Port in Harare is the centre of the Zimbabwe economy where US Dollars and South African Rands are traded. We call them, 'Moving Banks'. Goods are smuggled into the country without paying duty. There is no governmental control, over the economic backbone of the country.

ECONOMIC STRUCTURAL ADJUSTMENT PROGRAMME FOR ZIMBABWE

The economic status going down started soon after the introduction of the Economic Structural Adjustment Programme (ESAP), which was introduced by the International countries. This ESAP did not help Zimbabwe at all; actually it destroyed the economy of the country instead of building it. It became a loophole **for those who were on the upper-**hand of the projects which were being implemented. They were reports of projects being carried out in the development of the rural areas and the infrastructure of the towns.

Prior to the creation of the state of Zimbabwe official trade unions in Rhodesia were largely controlled by the white minority and worked to preserve the economic privilege of white workers over the black majority. While trade unions representing the black majority workforce did exist, their activities were hampered by the racially-discriminatory Rhodesian government, and their close association with the Black Nationalist movement meant they were relatively inactive during the Rhodesian Bush War. Trade union membership increased rapidly following the establishment of majority-rule government in 1980, and reached approximately 200,000 in 1985. The number of strikes and industrial disputes also increased dramatically, against the wishes of the new government. It was to combat this trend that the government established the ZCTU, as well as promising the introduction of a minimum wage and limited industrial democracy.

The initial leadership of the ZCTU was politically closely associated with the government, and was dismissed in 1984 for corruption.[4] Their replacements (following a period of caretaker administration) were also found to be corrupt, with the General Secretary removed for misappropriating funds in November 1986.[4] The direction of the ZCTU changed dramatically after the appointment of Jeffrey Mutandare, of the Associated Mineworkers' Union.[4] Mutandare was much more willing than previous leaders to criticise government policy, including the new Labour Relations Act of 1985, which he claimed centralised control over the trade union movement in the Ministry of Labour.

In the 1990s the ZCTU grew increasingly opposed to the government of Robert Mugabe due to the government's pursuit of neoliberal economic policies, as well as perceived government corruption and authoritarianism. At its 1995 Congress the ZCTU launched a major economic policy statement, 'Beyond ESAP', criticising the Mugabe government's adoption of the Economic Structural Adjustment Programme (ESAP). The ESAP involved the introduction of neoliberal macroeconomic policies, at the encouragement of the World Bank. The ZCTU was the main force behind the formation of the opposition party, the Movement for Democratic Change, established in 1999. The Secretary-General of the ZCTU, Morgan Tsvangirai, later became the President of the MDC.

By the end of the 1980s there was increasing agreement amongst government elites that new economic policies needed to be implemented for the long-term survival of the regime. The new policy regime designed by the government and its advisers[8] set out to encourage job-creating growth by transferring control over prices from the state to the market, improving access to foreign exchange, reducing administrative controls over investment and employment decisions, and by reducing the fiscal deficit. It had wide local support and was introduced before economic problems had gone out of control. A 40% devaluation of the Zimbabwean dollar was allowed to occur and price and wage controls were removed.

The austerity plan in Zimbabwe was followed by economic problems of increased severity. Growth, employment, wages, and social service spending contracted sharply, inflation was not reduced, the deficit remained well above target, and many industrial firms, notably in textiles and footwear, closed in response to increased competition and high real interest rates. The incidence of poverty in the country increased during this time. On the positive side, capital formation and the %age of exports in GDP increased and urban–rural inequality fell.

The new policies were undermined by extremely unfavourable conditions. Drought reduced agricultural output, exports, public revenue, and demand for local manufacturing. Growth during three drought-affected years (1992, 1993, and 1995) averaged 2.6%; during three good years (1991, 1994, and 1996) it was 6.5%. The new ANC regime in South Africa cancelled its trade agreement with Zimbabwe at this time and subjected its exports to punitive tariffs, just as Zimbabwe reduced its own, contributing significantly to deindustrialisation.

The government's failure to bring the fiscal deficit under control undermined the effectiveness of those elements in the program that were followed through. This led to growth in public borrowing, sharp increases in interest rates, and upward pressure on the exchange rate just as local firms were exposed to intensified foreign competition. Many firms failed, many others were forced to restructure, and new investment was discouraged in both the formal and increasingly important informal sector. The limited cuts that were made concentrated on the social services and led to serious reductions in the quality of health and education.

The government's austerity plan coupled with a relatively weak and highly protected economy came far too quickly. Uncompetitive industries were eliminated and over manning was reduced, but in such a sudden and disruptive manner as to cause economic chaos. Similar problems occurred in certain Eastern European countries after the collapse of Communism. The government's management of the transition to capitalism was much better. The public reaction to the disaster only further undermined the economy perpetuating a vicious cycle. By the mid-1990s, there were signs of improvement. However, the patience of both the government and the people were exhausted, and a new direction was taken.

In 1998 Mugabe's intervention in the civil war in the Democratic Republic of the Congo (Kinshasa)-purportedly to protect his personal investments-resulted in suspension of international economic aid for Zimbabwe. This suspension of aid and the millions of dollars spent to intervene in the war further weakened Zimbabwe's already troubled economy. In part through its control of the media, the huge parastatal sector of the economy, and the security forces, the government has managed to keep organised political opposition to a minimum through most of the 1990s.

By 1990 there were increasing demands for greater native African participation in ownership of the economy on the basis of continuing racial inequalities in the post-colonial economy. For example, by 1991, 50% of the population received less than 15% of total annual incomes and about 15% of total consumption, while the richest three% of the population received 30% of total incomes and were responsible for 30% of total consumption. The government-controlled economy of the 1980s tried to redistribute wealth to the black majority while emphasising racial harmony. With the increasing economic problems at the end of the 1990s and the reforms of the 1990s, new complaints were heard about the unequal racial distribution of wealth. For the ruling party, there was also a political imperative as the emergence in the late 1980s of opposition parties such as the Zimbabwe Unity Movement and the Forum Party had demonstrated the potential for political opposition from disconcerted sections of the African middle class. This emphasis on redistribution of wealth from whites to blacks was a policy that the government began to directly pursue in the mid-1990s.

From 1991–1996, the Zimbabwean Zanu-PF government of president Robert Mugabe embarked on an Economic Structural Adjustment Programme (ESAP), designed by the IMF and the World Bank, that had serious negative effects on Zimbabwe's economy. In the late 1990s, the government instituted land reforms intended to redistribute land from white landowners to black farmers to correct the 'injustices of colonialism'. However, many of these farmers had no experience or training in farming. From 1999 to 2009, the country experienced a sharp drop in food production and in all other sectors. The banking sector also collapsed, with farmers unable to obtain loans for capital development. Food output capacity fell 45%, manufacturing output 29% in 2005, 26% in 2006 and 28% in 2007, and unemployment rose to 80%. Life expectancy dropped.

The Reserve Bank of Zimbabwe blamed the hyperinflation on economic sanctions imposed by the United States of America, the IMF and the European Union. These sanctions affect the government of Zimbabwe,[8] and asset freezes and visa denials targeted at 200 specific Zimbabweans closely tied to the Mugabe regime.[9] There are also restrictions placed on trade with Zimbabwe, by both individual businesses and the US Treasury Department's Office of Foreign Asset Control.

A monetarist view is that a general increase in the prices of things is less a commentary on the worth of those things than on the worth of the money. This has objective and subjective components:

• Objectively, that the money has no firm basis to give it a value.

• Subjectively, that the people holding the money lack confidence in its ability to retain its value.

Crucial to both components is discipline over the creation of additional money. However, the Mugabe government was printing money to finance involvement in the Democratic Republic of the Congo and, in 2000, in the Second Congo War, including higher salaries for army and government officials. Zimbabwe was under-reporting its war spending to the International Monetary Fund by perhaps $ 22 million a month.

Another motive for excessive money creation has been self-dealing. Transparency International ranks Zimbabwe's government 157th of 177 in terms of institutionalised corruption.[14] The resulting lack of confidence in government undermines confidence in the future and faith in the currency.

Economic miss-steps by government can create shortages and occupy people with workarounds rather than productivity. Though this harms the economy, it does not necessarily undermine the value of the currency, but may harm confidence in the future. Widespread poverty and violence, including government violence to stifle political opposition, also undermines confidence in the future.[15] Land reform lowered agricultural output, especially in tobacco, which accounted for one-third of Zimbabwe's foreign-exchange earnings. Manufacturing and mining also declined. An objective reason was, again, that farms were put in the hands of inexperienced people; and subjectively, that the move undermined the security of property.

Government instability and civic unrest were evident in other areas. Zimbabwean troops, trained by North Korean soldiers, conducted a massacre in the 1980s in the southern provinces of Matabeleland and Midlands, though Mugabe's government cites guerrilla attacks on civilian and state targets. Conflicts between the Ndebele ethnic minority and Mugabe's majority Shona people have led to many clashes,[17] and there is also unrest between blacks and whites, in which the land reform was a factor. An aspect of this reform that seeks to bar whites from business ownership induced many to leave the country. Lack of confidence the government practice a fiscal restraint feeds on itself. In Zimbabwe, neither the issuance of banknotes of higher denominations nor proclamation of new currency regimes led holders of the currency to expect that the new money would be more stable than the old. Remedies announced by the government never included a believable basis for monetary stability.

In 2007, the government declared inflation illegal. Anyone who raised the prices for goods and services was subject to arrest. This amounted to a price freeze, which is usually ineffective in halting inflation. Officials arrested numerous corporate executives for changing their prices.

In December 2008, the Central Bank of Zimbabwe licensed around 1,000 shops to deal in foreign currency. Citizens had increasingly been using foreign currency in daily exchanges, as local shops stated fewer prices in Zimbabwe dollars because they needed foreign currency to import foreign goods. Many businesses and street vendors continued to do so without getting the license.

In January 2009, acting Finance Minister Patrick Chinamasa lifted the restriction to use only Zimbabwean dollars. This too acknowledged what many were already doing. Citizens were allowed to use the US dollar, the euro, and the South African rand. However, teachers and civil servants were still being paid in Zimbabwean dollars. Even though their salaries were in the trillions per month, this amounted to around US$ 1, or half the daily bus fare. The government also used a restriction on bank withdrawals to try to limit the amount of money that was in circulation. It limited cash withdrawals to Z$ 500, 000, which was around US$ 0.25

Living with hyperinflation was a challenge for Zimbabweans. Prices in shops and restaurants were still quoted in Zimbabwean dollars, but were adjusted several times a day. Any Zimbabwean dollars acquired needed to be exchanged for foreign currency on the parallel market immediately, or the holder would suffer a significant loss of value. For example, a mini-bus driver charged riders in Zimbabwean dollars, but different rates throughout the day: The evening commute was highest-priced. He sometimes exchanged money three times a day, not in banks but in back office rooms and parking lots.

Such business venues constituted a black market, an arena explicitly outside the law. Trans actors could evade the price freezes and the mandate to use Zimbabwean dollars. The black market served the demand for daily goods such as soap and bread, as grocery stores operating within the law no longer sold items whose prices were strictly controlled or charged customers more if they were paying in Zimbabwean dollars.[35] At one point, a loaf of bread was Z$ 550 million in the regular market, when bread was even available; apart from a trip to another country, the black market was the only option for almost all goods, and bread might cost Z$ 10 billion

ZIMBABWEAN PERIOD

ECONOMIC AND POLITICAL STATUS OF ZIMBABWE

According to a 1995 World Bank report, after independence, "Zimbabwe gave priority to human resource investments and support for smallholder agriculture," and as a result, "smallholder agriculture expanded rapidly during the first half of the 1980s and social indicators improved quickly." From 1980 to 1990 infant mortality decreased from 86 to 49 per 1000 live births, under five mortality was reduced from 128 to 58 per 1000 live births, and immunisation increased from 25% to 80% of the population. Also, "child malnutrition fell from 22% to 12% and life expectancy increased from 56 to 64. By 1990, Zimbabwe had a lower infant mortality rate, higher adult literacy and higher school enrolment rate than average for developing countries".

In 1991, the government of Zimbabwe, short on hard currency and under international pressure, embarked on an austerity program. The World Bank's 1995 report explained that such reforms were required because Zimbabwe was unable to absorb into its labour market the many graduates from its impressive education system and that it needed to attract additional foreign investments. The reforms, however, undermined the livelihoods of Zimbabwe's poor majority; the report noted "large segments of the population, including most smallholder farmers and small scale enterprises, find themselves in a vulnerable position with limited capacity to respond to evolving market opportunities. This is due to their limited access to natural, technical and financial resources, to the contraction of many public services for smallholder agriculture, and to their still nascent links with larger scale enterprises."

Moreover, these people were forced to live on marginal lands as Zimbabwe's best lands were reserved for mainly white landlords growing cash crops for export, a sector of the economy favoured by the IMF's plan. For the poor on the communal lands, "existing levels of production in these areas are now threatened by the environmental fragility of the natural resource base and the unsustainability of existing farming practices". The International Monetary Fund later suspended aid, saying reforms were "not on track."

According to the World Health Organisation (WHO), life expectancy at birth for Zimbabwean men have since become 37 years and is 34 years for women, the lowest such figures for any nation.[49] The World Bank's 1995 report predicted this decline in life expectancy from its 1990 height of 64 years when, commenting on health care system cuts mandated by the IMF structural adjustment programme, it stated that "The decline in resources is creating strains and threatening the sustainability of health sector achievements".

While Zimbabwe has suffered in many other measures under Mugabe, as a former schoolteacher he has been well known for his commitment to education. As of 2008, Zimbabwe had a literacy rate of 90%, the highest in Africa. However, Catholic Archbishop of Zimbabwe Pius Ncube decried the educational situation in the country, saying, among other scathing indictments of Mugabe, "We had the best education in Africa and now our schools are closing". Prior to its suspension in 2009, the Zimbabwe dollar had suffered from the second-highest hyperinflation rate of any currency in modern times

Rhodesia was better and a beautiful country, people lived a normal life. There was a clear indication that if the talks between minority and the majority were to be carried out amicable life for everyone was going to be good on both sides. We who ran away for greener pastures could have been home and helping in developing our country. There were a lot of issues that needed the Rhodesian government to look into; economically Rhodesia was doing well. For the British who came and settled in our country, they developed our country. But the only issue they forgot the majority of the people or rather, they got carried away and forgot that one day they will be a wakeup call. They will want to reclaim their ancestors land and share it with them. This redistribution of land and wealth had to be done. How was this issue supposed to be solved? I think it needed to be addressed in a more professional way I assume that the International countries cannot comment on an action taken by the Zimbabwean government on farm invasion, I suppose it's an issue which was on hand, and they knew that one day blacks will revolt and claim their land.

As for the bush war in Zimbabwe it was based on the reclamation of the ancestral land. Zimbabwe can solve its own problems; I do not think so, no! My reading refers me to our ancestors who were being killed by the Impis, the Lobengula warriors. The Mashona use to run away and live by the mountains in caves and so forth. In this case we are now advanced we are able to board a plane and go abroad to start a new life. Land redistribution in Zimbabwe needed addressing in a very serious amicable way, because the white farmers displaced black Zimbabweans made them settle on barren land. They struggled to grow food for their consumption but they ended up failing to produce enough for their needs. People ended up working at a commercial farm nearby owned by a British settler. The set up for the Tribal Trust Lands near a commercial farm advantaged a white man in the context that cheap labour was provided by black people who lived in the villages nearby the commercial farms. People worked at the farms in order to sustain their families due to poverty. Their children would attend a school which was strategically built in the farm. The parents would work in the fields for food and school fees their children's education. They practically worked for nothing because they were offered a credit system that they always owed the farmer. They were given ration food from the farmer every week; a bucket of maize meal and half bucket of beans. Maize meal prepared (sadza) thick porridge to eat with beans. This set up of these credits disadvantaged the workers they never had money in their pockets. Part of their earnings goes to clear the credit, for the children's school fees the other for groceries which they would have taken from the small convenient shop which was built by the farmer owned by the farmer. Every month these men and women their take home was nothing. They had clothes like uniform because they had a society of their own the seamstress who worked for the farmer, sown their clothes fashion was a story tale.

They had this outstanding dressing code which quickly identified them from the rest of the people. I remember seeing some of them with these summer dresses which had gathers on the waist or box plaits. The colourful prints on materials were colour blinding but lasted only one wash. It was just that cheap material from the Indian shops down town Salisbury. The farmer would play his record player they had this type of music that I do not think I had ever heard it played in Harare were I was born. Their music was weird which was sung by the new imaging farm worker singers however it usually ended there, not on the music charts of Zimbabwe. The equal rights mechanism needed to be put in place and stop slave labouring. It was an issue which needed addressing in an amicable way rather than jumping into conclusions. I do feel for anybody who is a Zimbabwean who can be a thinker just like me can understand.

On the other hand, this land redistribution was blown out of proportion by being implemented at the wrong time. The timing were not right, it was not supposed to be used as a political weapon. The political situation in Zimbabwe has taken many turns the introduction of the opposition parties, the malfunction of the economy. The major towns' municipality failed to provide the basic needs. Things took a wrong turn funding for the services disappeared the residents were no more receiving the services they need e.g. garbage collection, burst water pipe not being repaired, sewage pipes broken and stay a week or more without being repaired, electricity supply for residents was no longer reliable. Electricity Load shading for households would go for days without electricity

The major issue in Zimbabwe was the deterioration of services and maintenance. Companies like (ZESA) Zimbabwe Electricity Supply Authority are the back-bone of the economy. When I look back I remember that the Rhodesian government left a project that was in place for the upgrading of the hydro-electricity equipment at the Kariba dam, Hwange (Wankie) power stations, and Harare central power station. The upgrading of the new generators was to add more power to Harare due to the fact that the town infrastructure was growing. The municipality of Harare and other major towns were in the progress of building houses for the people, and upgrading the small rural area townships in to town. This was an effort to try and reduce the migration of people into major towns. This was based on enabling people to have electricity even in rural area. There were new grinding mills which were electronically operated. Schools had to have electricity and new technologies were being put in place like computers. The rural areas schools were being upgraded, the rural areas hospitals were now having electricity; minor operations were now being able to be carried out. The rural areas township centres were now being upgraded to small village towns. Convenient shops had electricity, they had fridges, freezers and they were now in a position to sell cold drinks. Companies like Coca-Cola and Schweppes the soft drink providers, provided their designed fridges for the shops with their logo on them. All these services were to attract the local people in those areas. There was nothing they were going to go to major cities. The local authorities decided to build low cost houses for rent for the teachers and local government employees who were now working in the offices for the service, like birth / death certificates, identity cards applications and etc.

Let's get back to the more pressing issue, the new electricity generators. Just as well this was a plan for the rural electrification. It's just a concern, as a citizen from this country, Zimbabwe, which has gone from riches to rags; some say from rags to riches for us it's the other way round.

The water supply, what happened to the water supply of Harare? Now you find people have resorted to sink boreholes. People spend weeks without water. What started first were the smell of the water and the colour of the water that was coming through the house taps it was greenish or brown and had a stench smell.

Harare water is recycled water from Lake Mhanyame. When you open a water tap the whole house stink like sewage. The purification chemicals were no longer being used. People of Harare suffered dysentery; children were dying of stomach diseases. The municipality of Harare announced that the water is not fit for human consumption; the only way to drink the water was to boil it, cool it. Whilst you cool the water it had this residue which remained below the saucepan.

All these issues need to be addressed in favour of the people of Zimbabwe. I do agree that you cannot just build your house anywhere. The town planning infrastructure had already fallen apart it is easier said than done. Planning in Zimbabwe is just harp hazard it seems everything is based on political situation. Well the clean-up was long overdue especially in the urban areas particularly because the major towns were dirty and overpopulated? The township has been breeding thieves; some people were homeless and living by the bus station. People were meant to be resettled in a humane way not to be treated like animals. All this was due to the government's promises that this is where many people differ with the government that make promises today later they turn around, man handle people and throw them away in the bush people are treated like animals. Because moving people from one point to the other needs a lot of infrastructural planning. Most of the issues that arise in Zimbabwe are nerve raking. We do agree to the clean-up but we disagree in the time factor that these clean-up setting take place. People's views need to be considered, given time to move on. I sometimes wonder whether this is the government that people voted for or is it a one-man band, or a few of those other people. People of Zimbabwe need to solve their own problems with many help from the international countries.

The migration of people from Zimbabwe is enough to demonstrate that they were against the political, economic status in Zimbabwe. There is no other better way of demonstrating to the international countries I suppose.

I cannot believe Zimbabwe's shunt houses, are houses which are built using planks or plastics, it sounds like Zimbabwe is the first one on this earth to have such accommodation. We must admit these houses do use to accommodate thieves and they were not proper for people to live in those houses for health and safety reasons. The people are already suffering why add some more problems to them. Why is it that when people take their concerns to the streets (demonstrations) the government decisions just take a split second, people can be arrested and beaten. Why is it that there is no human respect? These people voted for this government, no wonder why people are disillusioned. Majority of people used to think there was a light at the end of the tunnel but they now live day by day. Poverty is the norm.

The Zimbabwe, "CLEAN-UP". What is this clean up and to what extent? Was there a consultation held with the people of Zimbabwe that voted for the Black Zimbabwean majority rule? The development of the country Zimbabwe was all thrown through the window. The socio-economic goals of Zimbabwe were forgotten; instead of thinking about how to develop our industrial and agricultural sectors and stop channelling everything to politics. Politics became the norm, there was nothing functioning without politics instead learning new technologies on how we can farm drought resistant products and have enough food reserves for those dry seasons, and also learn to new ways of farming following those who have the experience ploughing in dry lands? We were busy fighting against one another. Tribalism, what is tribalism in the world. Do we sit down and think of the children that we are bringing into this world under these circumstances. Hatred! What reason? I think some people were just born evil.

The importance of bringing human rights violators to justice was that it clearly demonstrated that it was a declaration that no one is above the law including those even the most powerful members of the state apparatus. For this reason, the obligation on the authorities to bring charges against those believed to have committed human rights abuse is even greater than when similar crimes are committed by ordinary citizens. Unfortunately, by means of indemnity regulations, amnesties and simple failure to prosecute, the Zimbabwean government has instead created the impression that certain agencies – notably the CIO, but on occasions branches of the police and army too – are a law unto themselves. The retention of torturers and other human rights violators in positions of authority and the failure to take action against them unmistakably suggest that the government does not regard such crimes as serious. They also greatly increase the likelihood that human rights violations will recur. The government's failure to take action against human rights violators also discourages individuals from complaining about abuses for fear that they will be further victimized.

The Zimbabwean Government has been criticized for failing to amnesty civilians imprisoned for "dissidents" offences, when it has released members of security forces who have committed similar or often more serious, crimes. This inconsistency reinforces the impression that members of the security forces and ruling party are not subject to the rule of law. Africa Watch urges the government to release all those serving sentences for "dissidents" offences under a general amnesty. They also urge that there be no future general amnesties for those responsible for human rights abuses and the government's intention to prosecute those of its servants who abuse human rights be clear and publicized for the people of Zimbabwe.

Africa Watch also urges the government to repeal the protection of Wildlife (Indemnity) Act, passed earlier that year, which protects game wardens from prosecution for abuses. They consider that this was likely to encourage such abuses as well as being contrary to the basic principle of equality before the law.

Payment of compensation was one of the most important remedies when agents of the state violate an individual's rights. The right to seek redress through courts is guaranteed in international human rights instruments. Yet, despite several rulings by Zimbabwean courts in favour of victims of abuse, the government has apparently never paid compensation

Africa Watch urged the Zimbabwean government to alter its practice in this regard and to make compensation payments to victims of human rights abuse, including unlawful detention and torture, as well as to the relatives of people who have "disappeared" or been victims of political killings by members of the security forces. Such payments should be made without prejudice to any other criminal or civil proceedings.

A precondition to both the prosecution of human rights violators and the payment of compensation to those whose rights have been abused is the prompt and impartial investigation of allegations of abuse. Under its Commissions of Inquiry Act Zimbabwe has the mechanism to conduct major investigations with most of the necessary guarantees of impartiality. Its major weakness is that it does not require investigations to be conducted publicly or to publish their conclusion. Thus, for example, a major commission of inquiry on human rights abuses in Matabeleland in 1983 reported to the government but its findings have never been made public. Although human rights investigations may occasionally have to proceed in private, the general rule should be that they are public in order to safeguard their impartiality.

There are two issues in particular still need inquiry. One is the unresolved question of "disappearances," both of prisoners held in police custody and of people abducted in rural areas of Matabeleland and Midlands, apparently by the security forces. The aim of such investigations would be to determine their whereabouts, to enable death certificates to be issued where appropriate, to facilitate the payment of compensation to their relatives and to prepare for criminal prosecution of those responsible for the "disappearances."

The second issue, which needs investigation, is the continuing use of torture, particularly by the CIO. The aim of such an investigation would be to establish the truth of continuing allegations of torture, to facilitate the payment of compensation to those who have been tortured and to prepare criminal prosecutions of those law enforcement officials alleged to have carried out torture. Pending criminal proceedings, they should be removed from their posts.

In addition, there should be a permanent mechanism whereby individual complaints of abuse can be investigated. By this means, a person who alleges that he or she has been tortured or that a relative has "disappeared" can have his or her complaint promptly impartially investigated. This might be achieved, by expanding the existing office of the ombudsman, who looks into complaints of maladministration. However, such a body should also have discretion to initiate inquiries when there has been no complaint, since there are many reasons why people who have suffered traumatic experiences such as torture may be reluctant to come forward to present their complaint.

Although it ratified the African Charter on Human and People's Rights in 1986, Zimbabwe is not part of any of the major United Nations human rights instruments. Africa Watch urges the Zimbabwean Government to begin moves to ratify the International Covenant on Civil and Political Rights (with its Optional Protocol) and the Convention against Torture or Other Cruel, Inhumane or Degrading Treatment or Punishment. Not only do these treaties give legal force to the human rights first codified in the Universal Declaration of Human Rights (of which the Zimbabwean Government has declared itself a staunch supporter); they also incorporate mechanisms for reviewing the adherence of states to the provisions of the treaties and investigating complaints from individuals who claim that their rights have been violated.

ZIMBABWEAN PERIOD

LEAVING MY BELOVED COUNTRY ZIMBABWE TO LIVE IN EUROPE

The reason why I left Zimbabwe unceremoniously was due to the fact that I was under pressure, due to the political unrest at the institute of higher learning where I was a lecturer. Students were demonstrating more frequently in other instances weekly. Within our classes we had the students' union leaders who were now in the MDC party. On each lecture I could find there was two or more additional student I have never seen before, but had no say to this. I lost control of my power as a lecturer my freedom of teaching was under surveillance of the government informers. I could not trust anyone, even some of the other lecturers were very much into reporting others, to the government. I felt very vulnerable, since I was a woman who had fought for her rights to be in the position I was in. I had joined the men's world some of colleagues' male lecturer's tried to be in charge of my department, but I was not having it. In this case I thank the principal who believed in me. I was so scared; my teaching was now suffering because I could not talk about anything that was related to the economy of the country. Teaching economics, one is bound to relate the subject to the current affair issues. After each lesson the student would confront me asking me questions about the country's economy, I used to reply that I hope things will get better. I was living in fear, just a knock at the door at home or at the work I would jump because of the fear of being taken to be locked up in prison for no apparent reason. It was really frustrating to think that, I was educated all I ever wanted was to part my knowledge to the future generation of Zimbabwe. I decided not to be hard on myself and try to do my job forget about all that was going on, but that was not meant to be. I suppose that was just a wish, the political situation turned worse, the educational institutes were now the playground for riot police wearing high heels was now out of fashion, had to have flat shoes or sport shoes. As for lecturers the salaries started to fail meeting the basic standards of living, those in the industrial areas were living below the poverty datum line. The moment I got my salary, paid the bills I was done, nothing left.

One day, I came to work as usual found students standing outside the class rooms in small groups. I went straight to my office got read for the lesson. My students followed me, and said to me, I think it will be better if, I could return to my office and lock myself up, before I could ask what was happening, the students started running towards the gate that lead to the town centre, shouting Ahoy! Ahoy! Ahoy! I sat in my office, within a short space of time I checked through the window, I could see the riot police chasing after the students with their rubber whips, throwing teargases towards them the smell of teargas was horrible. I had to go to the staff rest room to wash my face. When everything had calmed down the students had gone away some were arrested and others were not. On my way home, I was asked again to report to the police station; I went there I was questioned pushed against the wall spat at, kicked, and slapped across the face, until they decided to let me go. These types of scenarios of lecturers being taken and questioned about students continued for some time, until one day I decided that it was far too much for me, whatever happened let it be, I refused to go to answer the stupid questions about students' demonstrations about when are they taking place. I did not have any idea, besides the fact that I was their teacher.

The demonstrations increased by the day towards the referendum in 1998 the students started handing out red card which were indicating that people should vote Mugabe out, vote of no confidence, with the government. This referendum was held under the students' demonstrations and industrial sector was striking, the war veterans were asking for the money they were promised by the government to be paid to them. I remember vividly that I commented without thinking of my surrounding, I was coming from town centre, Harare. I was locked up for a week, they beaten the hell out of me, after that it made me much more vocal started spending my time in my relatives houses after work sleeping in different houses. After that I became a rebel they could not man handle me, because I would scream and my students could come to my rescue.

During the school holiday towards Christmas there was a teacher's union meeting followed by the Lecturer's forum which was held in Harare, where I met this British Diplomat, who asked me about my well-being and how I was coping working under the circumstances of being taken to be beaten, kicked and questioned about students demonstrations, by the police.

I started crying he held my hand and said I am here to help; he asked me if I needed any help, to save my life. He said he understood how much danger I was in. He informed me about my name being black listed. I nearly collapsed, I sat on the pavement. He was assisted by his fellow diplomat to lift me. I was sweating from my head down to my toes. They took me to my house. We got home, I asked them to come in, and they sat with me to work out on how they could help me, to get out of the country to come to England. One thing they told me was never to panic or show any signs that you want to leave or neither to about it to friends and family until such time. I had a tough time, I could not sleep, and I had night mares of the police coming for me. The only time I was confronted was why these two white men came to your house, of which I replied; I was not feeling well when I attended the forum, they gave me a lift home. They even visited my home whilst I was at work and questioned my maid, who was very rude to them and told them it was none of their business. She was such a strong person. I went to work as usual when the college opened after a long Christmas holiday.

Whilst I was at work, I got a call on my mobile phone to arrange a meeting with this diplomat. We had a meeting and I bought my ticket and arranged everything that was going to happen. On the day of my departure I went to work as usual. I had an evening flight to London that evening. I went say good bye to my mum my sister and brothers. I left, my mother was very happy, she prayed and blessed me. She thanked the diplomat for saving my life. She said that now she can be able to eat and sleep knowing that I was safe and living a life. I came here with a small suitcase, which carried a few clothes. I left everything that I had worked for, for years. My sister who was already here was waiting to meet me. I got here, at Heathrow airport, I was given six months to stay, and no questions were asked. I tried to look for the people who helped me, in Zimbabwe but I failed to locate them. Up to this day I thank them wherever they are. I registered to study a course, and my visa was extended for a year. But I was not comfortable with this college and extending visa once in a while issue.

I decided to seek asylum, I went to The Home Office of the United Kingdom and surrendered myself and told them I have failed to live like a ghost I want to have proper papers that will allow me to live freely and work normal without fear of being deported. I went to court, in Birmingham were I was placed in a hostel for asylum seekers and those with cases that needed to go to court. It was like a prison, it reminded me of prison, but this was better because there was no beating or kicking. We were well looked after, we were fed, we were clothed, we had bus passes, we had doctors, we had our case workers and asylum lawyers. When my first hearing at the court was arranged, I went to court with my lawyer, but it was unsuccessful. I was very upset; my lawyer said that it normally happens we will resubmit for a second hearing. The second hearing date was set for six weeks to come. I resorted to reading books whilst I was in the hostel, I could go for walks and read any book that I came across. My time came that I had to attend the court again; as usual I went feeling sick and hopeless. When we arrived we reported at the reception and were told which court room we were going to go to for my case. When we got in the court room, the presiding judge asked my lawyer, to present the case; he mentioned a few points, about my application to be allowed to stay.

There was also a home office lawyer who was there to talk about the home office regulations and why they were denying me to stay here in England. After the presentation of my case by my lawyer, the judge, asked me to stand for my case and why I was late to submit my application and what explanations I had, because I had all those qualifications and he was sure that I had a good understanding of the law. I told the judge that, there I was guilt beyond doubt that I acted very ignorant, and also because I was scared of being deported, due to the information I had heard through the media and papers about asylum seekers. Then he asked me what do you want now, I told him that I wanted to regulate my stay and be able to work for myself, my adopted children and my widowed mother. He just looked at me straight into my eyes, then said thank you I understand. The home office lawyer turned around and asked the judge if he could comment, the judge said go ahead, he requested me to repeat what I had said to the judge, but the judge refused me to repeat, because he asked him where he was all the time when the case was being presented. He wished me all the best and not to worry too much about my papers. I left feeling better than what I expected, I felt like a big load on my shoulder was removed. That day I went to bed and slept through the night. I had a lot of sleepless nights before the court.

Fortunately or unfortunately, I remember this vividly when I was in Zimbabwe, when my mother commented on my frequent visits, that is when I moved out and tried to live own my own. As usual, my Saturdays were to the township, back to my roots, back to mum's house at two-thirty in the afternoon on the spot, I will be opening the gate and mum would say "it is her" and yes really was me! One day my mum said to me, "It's you who went to live under those bright lights right at the heart of the town centre, the capital city where you can live on hamburgers and chips; why have you come to the township where we are living on vegetables and "sadza". It was embarrassing, but deep down I understood my mother had all the love for me, my not coming meant that I was starving in my rented flat. Well tell me who does not want to grow-up looked by after their mother. I would give her a few dollars today and tomorrow I am there to help her eat the food she will have bought with the money I had given her a few days ago. What an embarrassment!

I came to Europe with the help of people who managed to help me get out of Zimbabwe to save my life and also to live a normal life. The accusations were becoming unbearable, the students were demonstrating so much and everything was just out of control. They had a right to demonstrate, they were really focused on what they wanted the government to do, but the government was not having any of that; that's when the riot police will be unleashed to beat up the students and other workers who had joined in. Unleashing of the riot police was the worst part of it, because they would just beat the shit out of anybody they come across in that area of demonstration.

Well since I have been working very hard and thinking maybe, maybe I will get somewhere in life. However, one thing for sure I will not go there as long as there is no democracy. As an observer from afar the thing that I have observed is that Zimbabweans are keen observers of any poor condition economically, politically and they are not shy to take advantage of it when it shows weakness. I think now I understand politics better than before. I never expected anything along this line to happen to my country. Tell me who does not like Zimbabwe? Even British people still love our country, Zimbabwe. I managed to engage into my studies that I have always wanted computer studies. I do not know how things are going to work out. At present, I can manage to look after my mum without going back to help her eat the food she will have bought with the money that I will have send her.

When the economy of Zimbabwe started deteriorating, the young working force of Zimbabwe started to migrate. What would anyone expect people to do, besides to seek alternative solutions, leave the country? Zimbabweans started migrating to other countries, carrying their knowledge, which was needed for the development of the country, especially when the ministers in government started to personally use the monies that were intended for the development of the country. When the ex-combatants started claiming their compensation from the government as well, the economy of Zimbabwe really showed its cracks. That was a signal for the educated people to realise that they were not getting anywhere with this present government.

This is just an outburst of wishing things could have been good for Zimbabweans, than to have people disillusioned by the way the government funds were being misused. Moreover, did Zimbabwe try to maintain a good relationship with the International countries? No! Why? Who cares! Although when they look at the "colonization" all over especially Africa for its richness in minerals, the soil which was good for cultivation and there was life in Africa. There was no hurry in Africa, people are laid back and they do take it easy.

As a thinker these are my own views and opinions I suppose the administration of the country (Zimbabwe) failed to work due to the lack of some leadership knowledge or due to the leaders being self-centred not willing to learn because they a fought the war, yes, a very big Yes! Our brothers and sisters perished for this country but did that gave anyone to grind the country's economy to this state which it is in. On the other hand a country's economy is not based on personalising the country's economic issues but it needs support from every angle meaning from top to bottom then vice-versa. Not knowing that the repercussions were going to make the country go on an economic sliding down scale and no coming back. It's like a car without good brakes on a slop going down you cannot stop it because it will overturn you cannot risk that but you just hold on and pray for a miracle to happen, no reverse! That is the economic status of our country Zimbabwe today. Prices on basic commodities are sky rocketing.

Many people were misled on the understanding of independence of our country. Many Zimbabweans thought that it was leisure time not knowing that we actually needed to work twice as much in order to achieve our goals to have a strong economic background. You find that most people started stealing long time ago; it was more of a habit. Moreover, people started to look at where do you come from, why should you have such a post when no one from you area was a minister or a prominent supporter of the current ruling part. Bureaucracy creped in slowly and it was openly exposed. The other issue which was really sad was the Grain Marketing Board (GMB), when all the maize that was supposed to be meant for people was sold to the neighbouring countries. Who remembers the Paweni's story? He sold all the maize and pocketed all the monies.

Well this is a very sad story about Zimbabwe; we used to laugh at Zambia, Malawi, Mozambique, Ethiopia, you name it. Tell me where are we now? We are scattered all over the world as lost cattle no one trying to find us besides setting our minds on the consoling fact that, "I am in Europe and life is going on well for me". I think we need to go back to the drawing board start all over again. Let us try to find ourselves remember there is no place like home. We are very educated people but we lack this other thing called, "Togetherness". We do not feel for one another. Do you remember our freedom fighters' words – 'children of the soil'!

Do you remember the father of Zimbabwe, the true leaders who were not going to let us down? Because their love of people was greater than you can think, it was there but time was not on their side in life. There was always a disturbance when they try to come up with something to construct our country. Therefore if you are not observant I want you to try to look at all the people you emulate tell me what you see in their eyes their personality "eyes don't lie", take my word.

Us walking on this earth, are we the god's saints who want to preach the political gospel of Zimbabwe. By the look of it we can talk in our small gatherings, have a lot to say, but do we take it further than that besides saying. "I am not political". Well I suppose our fellow British did not understand the reason behind Zimbabweans coming to this country. On the other hand it showed solidarity or patriotism of black and white Zimbabweans protesting against what was and is happening in the country. It rather confuses me in a way. Nevertheless I think my confusion is in the way we are confused, we do not know what we want. The colonisation also played a major role because Zimbabweans are laid back people, very docile; mannerism is the same as the British.

I have returned to my research now, reflecting at practical issues; I am being my old self-observant. Observing from afar I have been working with my fellow citizens of Zimbabwe when you listen to their conversation it is more of money nothing else. People do hard work I have seen it with my own eyes. They do not have a life they do not even know where they are coming from or going. A conversation that you can have with them is only to talk about money well I tell you I do not work like that because it is not necessary. I look at what they have achieved in life nothing so why bother.

They only know how to blame other people nothing more. If you try to talk the political and economic status of our country they are a bit interested and want to know if some change has happened, but they can switch their mind off and let it go quicker than you expect. They work day in day out. This has become a playground for families breaking-up for more divorces than you can think of. Women are now becoming bigamists a husband here in England another one in Zimbabwe, just as well men do the same. Married woman put up with British men trying to run away from paying rent and bills. Others are strippers in the streets at night so that they can be able to get money to send home. Some are HIV positive dying each day if not spreading it, Unbelievable! Others are doing very well changing their professions to better ones, which enable them to work for their families. These are serious professionals earning a good salary have a very good life with their wives or husbands.

Others are struggling in the right direction advancing their previous professions they have a hope that things will change one day then we will go back home. Heard that saying," Human beings are the last species on earth and the worst". This is true, let us look at the respect of human nature in general people are dying each day endless wars. I have been thinking which other country in Africa that never had a problem politically neither economically. Which country is not having political, social and economic problems? Well it seems one way or the other we have had a fair share of it all as blacks just as well-being from the black continent of Africa.

In this land of survival of the fittest were qualifications are long forgotten only survival of the fittest is the norm, the routine of life style in Europe. I have been observing my fellow Zimbabweans since some of us were not doing any manual labour at home it seems we cannot catch-up with our fellow citizens. I mean some of us who had managerial posts and director's you name it. In this land of survival you are all at par it is highly likely that they get more than you, they can work 60-80hours a week.

What I enjoy mostly than anything is to sit and watch how others struggle to try to catch up with those who had jobs in the heavy industrial areas. I am fortunate that I grew up working hard. In my family we used to do all the jobs in the form of labouring. A big thanks to my mother for that I used to think she was a bad mother. I have learnt that she was a woman with a focus about the future of her off springs. I have worked on a production line, where timing is a paramount important. Some people kept on asking the supervisor to be transferred from one point to the other because they are able to cope. The jobs are very tiring and brain draining. Have you ever wet your bed be careful you might. Some have mistaken their handbags for a toilet wet in there at night just because the handbag was white. Some have slept walking to work thinking it was in the morning they were supposed to go to work whilst it's night time. The weather here is different you cannot tell sometimes people get disoriented to situations. Confusion of days dates place of work due to working hard in so many places chasing after the pound. They confuse their work place go to a different place only to be told you are not booked. Sometimes I think there are many people who are now in a state of confusion I hope it is not a disease. Fatigue is the norm of the day. What else can one do besides to sacrifice their life in order for the family at home to survive?

Soon after independence there was a lot that happened so fast, so much that to those who were slow to move they were left behind, practically they missed the freedom train: just get on board, no questions asked, at that moment thinking was not necessary. Black African people started to qualify for mortgages for posh houses in the white suburban areas that were previously owned by the white people. Our kids were now enjoying the white people's schools. The facilities were wonderful very well equipped. We had what we never had before. Black man for a headmaster or headmistress in a multi-racial school; at that moment we were mixed and everything seemed to be blending in well.

ZIMBABWEAN PERIOD

REFLECTIVE ACCOUNT OF
THE POLITICAL ISSUES IN ZIMBABWE

Everything was a dream that had come true for every Zimbabwean! Hey! It was more of a prestige to be asked where your kids are going to school, you say, "Prince Edward" with that English accent that we had acquired; people used to call it, "nose brigade" we felt we were more British than the British themselves. People preferred to buy their groceries by the town centre supermarkets; those days the upmarket departmental stores like, TM and OK Zimbabwe you name it. It was very trendy after shopping; you get in a taxi to go as far as Highfield, which was more than 20 miles.

A few years' later signs of deterioration to a number of services started showing, like the maintenance of government buildings, the government employees, those in uniforms, and their uniforms had faded and torn. Before independence these building were very well maintained, and servicing was always in place. Due to the fact that now the school restrictions were removed, but they remained as group 'A' schools, Most of the black people who now had their children in the group 'A' schools depending on their financial status.

Let us get back to the historical events of our country Zimbabwe. Before independence Mugabe's ZANU-PF made clear its intentions that Zimbabwe should be a one-party state. The independence construction agreed with Britain at Lancaster House in 1979 guarantees the preservation of a multi-party political system until 1990 – 10 years after independence, unless all members of parliament agree to it. There was never a clear demonstration of one party state in Zimbabwe because it is unachievable. There are a lot of misunderstandings with the people of Zimbabwe and the opposition parties. This could have been achieved if the political and economically status of the country was being carried out transparently and people were respected as human being and their rights were met.

Life is what happens to you, while you are busy making other plans. Whilst there still was no way to express my feelings about the deteriorating political and economic situation in Zimbabwe, I left the country that I loved dearly, my heart aches, and I had to leave to save my life. There are times when I had to refrain from writing this book due to feeling very uncomfortable with some of the issues that I have come across through my reading and researches about my country Zimbabwe. It makes me wonder, what was going on in my country. I sometimes feel sick, very worried my trust of anybody who is a Zimbabwean gets slimmer and slimmer each day. Due to the fact that, I do not know who is who at this present day and age. However, the fact is somewhere somehow, for the sake of the future generation one has to write about the atrocities that were caused by these manmade disasters of a country called Zimbabwe, the small jewel of Africa, what was not there in Zimbabwe.

Stories of this country called Zimbabwe, since the formation of (ZUM) Zimbabwe Unity Movement. The leader of ZUM is a former secretary-general of ZANU-PF, Edgar Tekere. Tekere was removed from the party and government posts in 1981 after his acquittal on a technicality murdering a white farmer the previous year. However, Tekere remained influential among the left wing of the ruling party and particularly in his home are of Manicaland on the eastern border, where he was provincial party chairman. He criticized corruption and the size of government, as well as increasingly distancing himself from the move towards a one-party state. In early 1988, he was removed from the leadership of ZANU-PF in Manicaland. Then, in October 1988, he made a speech fiercely attacking government corruption. However, he went a step further than any previous critics did by placing some of the blame on Mugabe for failing to remove corrupt members of government. The Central Committee of ZANU-PF promptly voted to expel him.

The episode was revealed because the defenders of single-party systems argue that criticism can be contained and encompassed within the framework of the ruling party. Yet here was a demonstration that as soon as anyone overstepped an invisible line he would be removed. This was not intrinsically surprising: as early as 1985, a group of ZANU-PF trade unionists who criticised corruption among their union leadership were detained for some weeks. However, Tekere's expulsion did as much as any single episode to illustrate to ordinary Zimbabweans the dangers of the one-party state.

Tekere did not instantly follow the advice of his followers, who included a vocal group of students at the University of Zimbabwe, and set up a new party. By the time he finally did, Mugabe had made his own moves against corruption and taken some of the wind out of Tekere's sails. Publicly the ruling party declared itself unconcerned by the formation of ZUM, although many column inches in the government press were devoted to the new party has alleged links to die-hard Rhodesians and South Africa.

However, despite their professed indifference, the authorities instantly began a sustained campaign of harassment against ZUM. The first two months of its existence were particularly sensitive because they coincided with a parliamentary by-election in Harare's Dzivarasekwa constituency, which ZUM contested. The ZANU-PF candidate was declared to have won, with ZUM polling 28% of the votes cast. Tekere alleged that two government ministers had illegally entered polling stations to intimidate voters, and that party loyalists had been bussed in from outside the constituency to vote. Africa Watch could not confirm these allegations. However, there must be serious doubts about the fairness of the election campaign. The police banned the first two ZUM election meetings at Highfield and Mabvuku – the first public meetings in the party's history. A subsequent rally in Chitungwiza was called off because ZUM supporters were locked out of the stadium where it was to be held. The chairperson of Chitungwiza Town Council, Forbes Magadu, said that the gates were locked because ZUM had not paid a deposit. The

Forbes Magadu is also ZANU-PF political commissar for Harare and plated a prominent part in the Dzivarasekwa campaign. At the same time security officials prevented members of the public from attending a meeting to launch ZUM in Bulawayo, and a ZUM official was subsequently charged with convening a public meeting without authority. A ZUM official also alleged that the managing director of the official Zimbabwe Newspapers had stopped an advertisement for a later ZUM rally in Bulawayo from appearing in the Chronicle newspaper.

On June 6, 1989 a prominent ZUM member Freddie Madenge was arrested in Harare. Davison Gomo, a senior party spokesperson, Lazarus Matungwazi, James Dziva and 11 other members were arrested two days later. They were held without charge at Harare Central Police Station. Unusually, Home Affairs Minister Moven Mahachi responded publicly to Africa Watch appeals on behalf of the 15 detained ZUM members:

"There is freedom to form political parties but there is no freedom to subvert a legitimate Government. We will not hesitate to pick anybody up as long as we have reasonable grounds that they are engaged in subversive activities."*

In fact, the 15 were released a few days later without charge, suggesting that the grounds for detaining them were not so reasonable. On July 18, 1989, Tekere was still trying to address his first public meeting since ZUM's formation. That evening armed police dispersed 500 students who were attending a rally addressed by Tekere at the University of Zimbabwe. Police fired teargas into students' dormitories. On October 6-7, 1989, 11 ZUM members were arrested in Chinhoyi, some 70 miles from Harare. They included the party's provincial secretary for Mashonaland West, Cornelius Watama. At the time of writing, they had apparently not been charged and had not seen a lawyer. A ZUM spokesperson also alleged that a store owned by a party supporter had been stoned by members of the Youth League of the ruling party.

When a newly formed party can win nearly a third of the vote in ZANU-PF's Harare stronghold, President Mugabe may take this as evidence that the public is not yet won over the idea of the one-party state. However, it was worrying that in the first two months of the new party's existence it suffered repeated harassment and detentions. The government was apparently unaware of any contradiction between this and its verbal assurances that anyone is free to form a political party.

A development, which concerned some observers, was the transfer of responsibility for the Youth Wing and Women's League of the ruling party away from the relevant Ministries (Youth, Sport and Culture and Community and Women's Affairs) into the Ministry of Political Affairs. The fear was that in the period leading up to the next general election in 1990 these wings of the will be engaged in violence and intimidation of political opponents. Such fears are not fanciful, since this was precisely what happened around the last general elections in 1985. Supporters of ZAPU were forcibly bussed to ZANU-PF rallies, beaten up, had their homes burned down and in few instances they were killed.*

Members of the Youth Wing were among those released under the June 1988 presidential amnesty. In September 1988, the Attorney General instructed the prosecution to drop all charges during trial of 13 youths from the ruling party alleged to have burned down and destroyed property owned by ZAPU members. The inference is that the government treats such behaviour lightly. In a plural society, it is highly questionable whether such party bodies should fall under the control of any Ministry; at elections time it creates the appearance that supposedly impartial state organs are favouring one party against others.

Those who criticise from outside the framework of party politics scarcely fare better than members of minority parties do. In September 1988, students at the University of Zimbabwe and Harare Polytechnic attempted to organise a demonstration against corruption. However, the police prevented the demonstration from leaving the campuses and broke up the protests with teargas and baton charges. The demonstrators declared their loyalty to President Mugabe and were taken aback when he returned from an overseas trip to endorse the harsh police action. Law lecturer Shadreck Gutto, a Kenyan political exile, was summarily expelled from the country because he was alleged to have helped the students draft an anti-corruption manifesto. Four other lecturers, along with six students, were charged under the Law and Order (Maintenance) Act with inciting public violence. The charges were later dropped, but the 15 members of the University Students' Representative Council had their grants withdrawn by the government in January 1989, apparently because they had circulated documents, which were said to be offensive to the office of the President.

Two months later the grants were restored after the students wrote a letter of apology to the Minister of Higher Education. In many respects the withdrawal of the grants was a more serious sanction than the criminal charges. To cut off the students' means of livelihood was a harsher penalty than anything the courts were likely to impose. In addition, the criminal charges were unlikely ever to succeed in court, whereas the withdrawal of the grants was an administrative measure for which the authorities were not required to give a reason. The calculated humiliation of the students by their letter of apology does not enhance either intellectual freedom at the university or political freedom in the country at large.

In June 1989, one of the four lecturers, who had been charged, Kempton Makamure, acting Dean of the Faculty of Law, was arrested and detained for a week at Harare's Marimba police station. The Emergency Powers (Maintenance of Law and Order) Regulations require that written reasons for detention must be served within seven days of a person's arrest. Since Makamure was released just within that time limit, the reasons for his detention were never officially stated. Apart from his alleged involvement in the anti-corruption protest, Makamure had offended the government in May 1989 when he gave a radio interview to the official Zimbabwe Broadcasting Corporation criticising the country's new investment code. Because the code, which liberalised foreign exchange requirements for overseas companies and facilitated the repatriation of profits, was generally welcomed in

Western economic circles but criticised by the Zimbabwean left. The two journalists who interviewed Makamure, Robin Shava and Nyika Bara, were suspended from their posts.*

On September 29, 1989, students at the university attempted to hold a seminar to mark the first anniversary of their anti-corruption demonstration. Some 200 riot police and CIO members arrived on campus to disperse 300 students, telling them that their gathering was illegal. On October 2 1989, the Students' Representative Council (SRC) issued a statement protesting the police action as a violation of academic freedom. In the early hours of October 4, 1989, police again came onto the campus to arrest Arthur Mutambara, SRC president, and Enoch Chikweche, the organization's secretary general. Mutambara was injured trying to escape arrest. As news of the arrests spread, thousands of students assembled to protest, according to reports in the government-owned press. In the course of this spontaneous demonstration, a Mercedes Benz car belonging to Vice-Chancellor Walter Kamba was damaged. At least 70 students were arrested. Later the same day Professor Kamba announced that the university was being closed indefinitely, the first time this had happened since independence in 1980. Kamba, who is known to be a close advisor of Mugabe, refused to condemn either the initial police action against the seminar or the arrest of the student union officials. Students were given only a few hours to leave the campus. The term had only just started and students had not yet received their grant payment, so many were stranded in Harare with no money. The closure, carried out in consultation with President Mugabe who is chancellor of the university, drew condemnation from the University Teachers' Association and the University Senate. Most of the students arrested on October 4 had been released by the end of the week, but six remain in detention at the time of the writing. Apart from the two SRC officials, they are Christopher Giwa, Peter Myambo, Edmore Tobaiwa and Samuel Simango. They were apparently held under the 30-day detention orders issued under the Emergency Powers (Maintenance of Law and Order) Regulations at various police stations in the Harare area.

Following that, there was the labour right's issue. Trade union rights, particularly for the black majority, were severely curtailed before independence. There has been a significant growth in trade unionism since 1980 and the emergence of a single trade union confederation, the Zimbabwe Congress of Trade Unions, which was often critical of government policy. However, under the 1985 Labour Relations Act the right to strike remains limited by lengthy negotiating procedures which must be exhausted before a strike can be regarded as legal.* the most serious threat to workers' rights lies in the prohibition under several different laws, including the Labour Relations Act, of the right of workers in "essential services" to withdraw their labour.

As in other areas, the Zimbabwean Government inherited repressive laws enacted by the Rhodesian regime, which it has since added to. The Emergence Powers Act defined essential services as hospitals, transport, electricity, water, sewerage, food fuel, coal fire brigade, coal mining and communications. These can be widened by notice in the Government Gazette. A notice of 1965, which is still in force, defines all finance, commerce and industry as essential services. The Law and Order (Maintenance) Act, dating from 1960, prescribes a maximum of five-years prison sentence for incitement to strike in an essential service (section 32) and ten years for interfering with an essential service (section 34).

In May 1989, junior doctors went on strike throughout the country in protest at pay and conditions of service. Many were arrested and 77 of them charged under sections 32 and 34 of the Law and Order (Maintenance) Act, although charges were later withdrawn after Mugabe himself had intervened to defuse the situation. However, as an apparent consequence of the doctors' strike, the government introduced new regulations under the Emergency Powers Act, which like the Law and Order (Maintenance) Act, outlaw strikes in "essential services." Since the definition of essential services in force is still that of the 1965 government notice, in effect any worker who goes on strike can be charged under the Emergency Powers (Maintenance of essential Services) Regulations, 1989, and will face a prison sentence of up to two years.

In August 1989, the new regulations were tried out for the first time against striking railway artisans. Then technicians at the Posts and Telecommunications Corporation (PTC) in Harare went on strike over a pay grievance. Telecommunications workers elsewhere in the country began a go-slow. By the first week in September, 116 PTC employees had been arrested and charged with breach of the new regulations. The lawyer for some of the accused argued that the regulations were in breach of the constitutional provision prohibiting forced labour.

As with the use of detention without trial, this appears to be an abuse of the use of emergency powers. The striking telecommunications workers have no connection with either the insurgency in Manicaland or South African espionage – the two stated reasons for maintaining the emergency. One leading PTC striker, Lovemore Matombo, was detained for a week under the Emergency Powers (Maintenance of Law and Order) Regulations and released just before the authorities were required to provide written reasons for his imprisonment.

After the closure of the university on October 4, the Zimbabwe Congress of Trade Unions issued a statement condemning the act of the Vice-Chancellor and government, under the name of its general secretary Morgan Tsvangirai. On the morning of October 6, the CIO arrested Tsvangirai; later that day he was taken, barefoot and handcuffed, to his office, which the CIO officials proceeded to search. He was taken away and, at the time of writing had not been seen again. On October 11, the High Court issued an order compelling the CIO to give Tsvangirai's lawyer access to him within 24 hours. Shortly after Tsvangirai's arrest, two other senior union officials were briefly detained for questioning. They were Andrew Ganya, organising secretary of Plastics, Chemical and Allied Workers Union and Trust Ngirande, organising secretary of the National Leather workers' Union.

* In 1987 the government's Secretary for Labour is reported as saying: "All strikes since I took office have been illegal because I have not approved any strikes." Cited by Brian Wood, "Trade

Union Organisation and the Working Class" in Colin Stoneman (Ed), Zimbabwe's Prospects, Macmillan, London 1988.

Let me take you back again to the honeymoon period of Zimbabwean independence. Huh! The other issue that issue was the Lancaster talks and how it influenced the change of the government, and how we over looked at what was discussed and what ended up happening. The three-month long conference almost failed to reach an accord due to disagreements on land reform. Mugabe was pressured to sign and land was the key stumbling block. Both the British and American governments offered to buy land from willing white settlers who could not accept reconciliation (the "Willing buyer, Willing seller" principle) and a fund was established, to operate from 1980 to 1990.

ZIMBABWEAN PERIOD

STORIES OF THE MASS MEDIA OF ZIMBABWE

The issue of Freedom of the press in Zimbabwe, in February 1989 Geoffrey Nyarota editor of the official Chronicle newspaper in Bulawayo found himself promoted to the newly created post of group public relations officer in Harare. The Chronicle had exposed a major corruption in which government ministers were buying cars from Harare's Willow vale assembly plant and reselling them at vast profit above the legal controlled price. As a result, President Mugabe set up a judicial commission of inquiry, which led to the resignation of several ministers.

Nyarota's deputy at the Chronicle, Davison Maruziva, was also promoted to become deputy editor of the Herald in Harare, which has been uncritical of any aspect of government policy or behaviour. The Chronicle has published no more corruption scoops under its new editor, Stephen Mpofu.

Under Nyarota and Maruziva, the Chronicle had provided chapter and verse for the allegations of corruption made by the students and Edgar Tekere. They were immensely popular and difficult to sack. Instead, they were subjected to what one backbench Member of Parliament called "elimination by promotion."

Almost inevitably, the Willow vale car scandal was dubbed "Willow-gate." It became known quite by accident in October 1988. Bulawayo businessman Obert Mpofu, who is also a member of parliament, received an unexpected cheque for nearly $ 4,000 from the Willow vale Company. It was actually intended for one Alford Mpofu, an employee of Mmnilal Naran who is a close friend of the then Industry Minister Callistus Ndlovu. (Naran had bought a $ 60,000 Bulawayo house for his friend, who was the minister responsible for the government-owned Willow vale plant. He was later arrested for foreign exchange offences.)

Alford Mpofu and another Naran employee, Don Ndlovu, had been allocated Mazda pick-up trucks from Willowvale on Naran's behalf. They had paid in advance but when they went to collect them, Mpofu had been allocated a cheaper model. Hence, the refund was sent to the wrong person, Mpofu.*

The exposure of "Willowgate" was not apparent intended to embarrass the government, since both the original source and the journalist responsible are thoroughly loyal to Mugabe. Obert Mpofu, a government member of parliament, took his story to Nyarota, a former Mugabe press secretary. The Chronicle pursued the affair vigorously over the weeks that followed, publishing lists of ministers who had been allocated Willowvale vehicles – and details of how these were resold illegally for two or three times the official price. Apart from Industry Minister Ndlovu, those implicated included two of Mugabe's most senior advisers: Minister of Defence Enos Nkala and Senior Minister for Political Affairs Maurice Nyagumbo.

Most Zimbabweans have a healthy scepticism towards the official news media, but retain a voracious appetite for real news. The Herald's dismissal record for serious reporting has led to a flourishing of independent news magazines such as Parade and Prize Africa, which mix sport, fashion and showbiz gossip with serious political journalism. The country's three daily papers, the Herald, the Chronicle and the Manica Post, are all government controlled, as are the Sunday Mail (Harare) and the Sunday News (Bulawayo) and two Shona and Sindebele weeklies. The weekly Financial Gazette is independent and critical, but has a small print run and is aimed largely at the white community.

The Catholic monthly magazine Moto is perhaps the most important forum for critical ideas. There is undoubtedly the market for a non-government daily newspaper with an independent editorial line. However, the existing dailies run at a loss and are heavily subsidised. There was no financial supporter prepared to incur the government's wrath by launching a new paper. Thus, the most important print media remain under effective government control. The radio, which is the most important news medium in a predominantly rural society with low-level literacy, is tightly controlled. Thus, the emergence of Nyarota's Chronicle as an investigative newspaper won it an enthusiastic readership in Harare, as well as Bulawayo. As the Willow vale story developed, long queues would form in the capital to wait the Chronicle's mid-morning arrival.

In November, the Chronicle was engaged in a further clash with government. A reporter, Gibbs Dube, accompanied by a driver named Phillip Maseko, visited the home of the governor of Matabeleland South, Mark Dube, to interview him about illegal gold-mining in Esigodini. (The two Dube's are not related.) The interview had been arranged by Geoffrey Nyarota. When they had seen the governor, Gibbs Dube and Maseko began the drive back to Bulawayo. Mark Dube's car overtook them and the governor and his security men flagged them down, seized their car keys and ordered them into his vehicle. They were driven to the governor's house. Gibbs Dube said afterwards:

The governor accused me of trying to discredit him. He accused me of publishing sensational news, which he said was not true. Then he started to assault me. He hit me twice with a clenched fist. He then tried to throw a beer bottle at me, but was restrained by one of the two men who were in the house. Then he left for his bedroom where he said he was going to fetch his gun to shoot me so that there would be big news to write about. He then came for me again, but his friends restrained him. Then he went for Comrade Maseko and started assaulting him with his fist. At that point, I ran away and escape.*

Maseko was handed over to the custody of the Esigodini police, who held him for some hours – while denying to the Chronicle that they had any knowledge of him.

All this was too much even for the management of Zimbabwe Newspapers. The group's chief executive, Elias Rusike, observed that if Mark Dube went unpunished, "Zimbabwe maybe entering a new frightening era when the rights of ordinary citizens are trampled underfoot willy-nilly by that in authority."** Likewise deputy commissioner of police Douglas Chingoka criticised police at Esigodini for detaining Maseko on Governor Dube's orders: "The police should protect people and should not get unlawful orders as no one is above the law,"***

Mugabe's reaction was quite different. He spent a press conference attacking "overzealous" reporters and repeating Mark Dube's extraordinary allegation that the two Chronicle men had gone to the governor's house secretly, disguised as gardeners. "A governor must be dignified," Mugabe said, "but this does not mean that there was no provocation."****

In September 1989, a Bulawayo magistrates' court found Governor Dube guilty of assault and fined him $ 150 at about the same time Joseph Polizzi, a reporter who had covered "Willowgate" for the Chronicle's sister paper, the Sunday News, narrowly escaped when a car drove at him as he left the office one night. He suffered bruising. Previously Polizzi had been arrested after he had dressed as a doctor in an attempt to enter Bulawayo city morgue to investigate a story. Polizzi alleges that he was assaulted and was suing the police. He was detained for eight days without charge.*

A fortnight after the Dube assault, Davison Maruziva telephoned Enos Nkala, the Minister of Defence, to seek his reaction to allegations that he was involved in the Willowvale racket. Nkala's response was quoted at length;

Where did you get that information? That information is supposed to be with the police and the president. I want that information here in my office. Who do you think you are?

If you do not travel here, (to Harare), I will teach you a lesson. I will use the army to pick you up and then you can ask your questions; I do not care ...

Do not play that kind of game with me. I am not Callistus Ndlovu. I am not the kind to play with. Play with anybody else. I am giving you ultimatum: if by tomorrow you do not come back to me to say you are coming, then you will come by other means.

I have the power. I will lock you up. Along with your editor who gave you that information. That question must be answered. I am the acting Minister of home affairs, I am instructing the police to search your offices, and you can write that. *****

From the safety of hindsight, this sounds like bluster. Nkala lied to the commission of inquiry into corruption and was forced to resign. At the time however, since the Minister of Home Affairs was out of the country, Nkala was in charge of both army and police. He threatened in 1986 that anyone who sent information to Amnesty International would be locked up. In addition, to prove that he meant it he ordered the detention of the head of Zimbabwe's leading human rights organization. Just two weeks beforehand, a member of the government had beaten up a reporter and apparently got away with it. Maruziva was entitled to feel scared. Nyarota later related, in sworn testimony to the commission of inquiry.

Some people came to warn us personally that this was no longer for us and in fact in due course the chairperson of the Zimbabwe Mass Media Trust (the major shareholder in Zimbabwe Newspapers) summoned me to Harare and indicated that reaction was very strong at this point from certain government ministers.

He told me he had called me up for my safety, that he understood that there were instructions that I should be first dismissed from work and subsequently arrested. He called me to Harare so that I would be safe here. I did confirm that Callistus Ndlovu, who; while the Information Minister had been away had been appointed acting minister, had issued instructions to the Zimbabwe Mass Media Trust that I should be dismissed immediately, which move the trust resisted.******

* The Herald, November 28, 1988
** The Herald, November 29, 1988
*** The Herald, November 30, 1988
**** Ibid.
***** The Chronicle, December 14, 1988
****** The Chronicle, January 27, 1989

At the end of December, Mugabe finally appointed a commission of Inquiry, headed by Justice Wilson Sandura, although there was still a widespread view that it would be a white wash. As it turned out, the commission held well-attended and highly theatrical hearings in Harare, where ministers such as Nkala and Ndlovu endured a merciless public inquisition. By the time the commission had reported, five ministers and a provincial governor had been forced to resign. One minister, Maurice Nyagumbo, committed suicide by drinking pesticide.

This should have been Nyarota's hour of glory. However, in January – shortly after the Sandura commission was established – information Minister Witness Mangwende announced his intention of "examining the structures" of the Mass Media Trust. Restructuring, it soon emerged, simply meant moving Nyarota and Maruziva where they do no harm. Nyarota was moved to a previously unheard of public relations job and Maruziva soon followed him to Harare. Formally, of course, these were promotions. But even Mugabe himself, seemed to have difficulty in getting his story straight. He said that no one would complain about getting a higher salary, but at the same time criticized Nyarota for "over zealousness." However, if Mugabe was uncertain whether Nyarota's removal was punishment or reward, the message conveyed to the public was clear Nyarota was promoted because he went too far.

Nyarota's removal aroused considerable public concern. Backbench Member of Parliament Byron Hove raised the matter in the House of Assembly. Ministers closed ranks, repeating the universal refrain of the government censor: they did not object the criticism, but it had to be constructive. Thus Sydney Sekeramayi, the Minister of State for National Security: "I want to stand here and make it very clear that some of us do not condone corruption, we are with it. But to the extent that the press now deliberately target Government as its enemy, then we part ways." (Zimbabwe: Parliament Debates, February 15, 1989)

In the course of his contribution to the parliament debate on Nyarota's removal, Byron Hove quoted from a pamphlet by Mikhail Gorbachev. "Criticism is a bitter medicine, but the ills that plague society make it a necessity. Those who think that criticism need only be dosed out at intervals are wrong. People who are inclined to believe stagnation has been fully overcome and it is time to take it easy are just as wrong. A slackening of criticism will inevitably harm glasnost and perestroika."*** A few weeks later Hove was advertised to address the Britain-Zimbabwe Society on the theme of "The need for glasnost and perestroika in Zimbabwe." The meeting never took place, after ZANU-PF Politburo member Didymus Mutasa had intervened to stop it.

Nyarota is the third editor to be removed from his post for offending the government. His removal, like the previous ones, raises important questions about who controls the press in Zimbabwe. At independence in 1980, the government, with the help of a Nigerian grant, bought out South African owners of the Herald, chronicle and Manica Post and their Sunday counterparts and set up a Mass Media Trust as principal shareholder in Zimbabwe Newspapers (1980) Ltd. The trustees are supposed to represent the people of Zimbabwe and trust objects strenuously when the newspapers are described as government-owned. However, in practice it is clear that the Minister of Information plays the decisive role in hiring and firing senior staff.

In July 1985 Elias Rusike, head of Zimbabwe Newspapers, wrote to Willie Musarurwa, removing him from the editorial chair at the Sunday Mail, Henry Muradzikwa, ran a story about Zimbabwean students being deported from Cuba allegedly because they were suffering from AIDS. The story coincided with the visit to Harare of a top Cuban official who objected to it. Mugabe publicly pledged, "I shall deal with him personally." Muradzikwa, like Nyarota, was removed to a non-editorial post. The Mass Media Trust does not seem to have been consulted.

On May 18, 1989 Robin Shava and Nyika Bara of the Zimbabwe Broadcasting Corporation interviewed Kempton Makamure on the new investment code for the Radio 4 program entitled "Gate." According to Byron Hove, who subsequently raised the matter in parliament, the following day the journalists were hauled up before Information Minister Mangwende and asked why they had "picked on Makamure who is in opposition to Government." In a letter from the Senior Controller of Radio Services, the two were suspended from duties with effect from May 23. (Zimbabwe: Parliament Debates, February 15, 1989)

Replying to Hove, Mangwende's Deputy Kenneth Manyonda made the customary disclaimer of government involvement in the suspensions, but then told the parliament, "it is not that Code should not be criticized, but that it should be criticized knowledgeably." He went on: "Any journalist who is worth his salt should know that there are two sides to any story, and considering that the Investment Code is what everybody was waiting for it was only proper for the press to play its role positively by giving those involved equal and ideally the first opportunity to inform and educate the public." (Zimbabwe: Parliament Debates, May 30, 1989) This was a curious comment, given that the press had spent the previous few weeks giving code enthusiastic mentions at every opportunity. The interview with Makamure was probably the first contrary view to be heard in the official media, Makamure's prior involvement with students' criticism was presumably not a coincidence. Hove pressed Manyonda on whether Shava and Bara were not in fact suspended because they held views critical of the government on the investment code issue. Manyonda would not confirm that the two journalists were summoned before the Minister on May 19 but did say that: All I am aware of is that when we listened to the tapes that involved the interviews on Radio 4 we were so perturbed that we brought the situation to the attention of ZBC management. What they did later, quite honestly we do not know. (Zimbabwe: Parliament Debates, May 31, 1989, 1989)

According to an unconfirmed report, Shava and Bara were later reinstated and, like Nyarota promoted out of harm's way. The exposure of "Willowgate" was an outstanding achievement by the young Zimbabwean press. It was able to occur largely because of the December 1987 unity agreement. The result has been a new era of political openness a breakdown in traditional party alignments. But now it appears that the opportunity for dissent was only temporary. The Chronicle has returned to bland predictability. The Herald, under Editor Tommy Sithole, continues to ignore financial scandals and to pour scorn on government critics. In April, after one particular partial Herald report about Edgar Tekere, a former political prisoner and veteran of the liberation struggle wrote an open letter to Sithole.

Lack of information and the absence of straightforward reporting are the direct causes of rumour-mongering. A pertinent example of this was the failure of the Herald to report Willowgate until the President announced the appointment of the Sandura Commission of Enquiry. This lack of reporting in the Herald was naturally widely commented on giving rise to the rumour that Tommy Sithole is himself implicated in Willow gate." … Without accurate and untarnished information, it is difficult for people to make correct decisions and this, at the end of the day, can damage the State … However, just as people demand and eventually get a certain standard in the conduct of Government, so people demand and eventually get a certain standard in the press that serves them. That is what the struggle for press freedom is all about.

**** Ibid (Zimbabwe: Parliament Debates, May 31, 1989, 1989)

Zimbabwe! We had all the basic necessities of a day-to-day life on the palms of our hands. What did we do about it? Whilst others were busy trying to build Zimbabwe others were busy with their five-pound hammers destroying it. It is like a caterpillar worms inside a maize cob you know what I mean when you think this year I will have a bumper harvest not knowing that someone inside hidden is doing a great job destroying what you have been expecting to be a high yield. What you will be left with is just an empty cob with nothing on it. Small land locked country Zimbabwe, with great mining and agricultural potential. Huh! Is it? Now they say Zimbabwe small country with the worst chaos, lawlessness, and corruption is the norm, no democracy, and no respect of human rights that is Zimbabwe! I never heard of a country that cannot stand opposition.

I used to think that if you have opposition in your parliament it will keep the ruling party on their feet trying very hard to put everything in order. The Zimbabwean government is more of eliminate the opposition. The clear fact is that Zimbabwe has many problems on hand no doctors, no nurses, no professionals, most of them ran away, decided to seek refuge in other countries. Where are you Zimbabwe my motherland, Zimbabwe! Children of the soil long left for greener pastures proud people Zimbabweans they could not swallow their pride with the teargases thrown at them when they expressed a political, or economic opinion by taking it to the streets, (demonstrations).

Which is supposed to be a democratic thing in a democratic country the riot police beat them for no apparent reason it was unbearable. I thought I should rewind my memory back take myself back from the beginning of the war of the Rhodesian black people liberalization. As an observer from afar I need to reflect and analyse things as they become clear in my mind elaborate them accordingly. It is important to elaborate otherwise the information will be misinterpreted or lose its meaning. Zimbabwe African Patriotic Union, which was formed by Joshua Nkomo, Josiah Chinamano, Ndabaningi Sithole, Chitepo, Parirenyatwa, Silundika, Takawira, Zvobgo, Muzenda and the rest.

Well history explains itself that black people organized mobilized a war that was against the oppression of the white minority rule of our country Zimbabwe. The oppression became obvious that people believed that this land belonged to the Majority people of Zimbabwe. There where comrades camp which were set in our neighbouring countries, Mozambique, Zambia, Tanzania. In addition other eastern European countries offered training for the freedom fighters, Young people started running away from home to go and fight this freedom for blacks' war. They went and settled in the neighbouring countries came in dodging the border posts patrolled by the Rhodesian soldiers to fight the war for the black majority rule.

There was an outcry sometimes when we used to hear that the Rhodesian forces bombed the camps and a number of youngsters have been killed. It was hard to think of it because youngsters used to run away from home without telling their fathers and mothers that we are going to the war. Bless them, for what they did for the sake of freedom. However one thing that has not been clear to the people of Zimbabwe was that the atrocities of the war the killings, the disappearance of people who were, and those who are vocal about the governance never stopped although the war ended.

People fought a tough war – people died in that war, they died! Young people who also wanted to enjoy the fruits of this country Zimbabwe. I still wonder what went wrong in the Promised Land which was said to be full of honey and milk the wishes of those who died for this country were they met I don't know? Black people of Zimbabwe never enjoyed democracy never had freedom of speech or expressing what they want their country to do for them. It is a pity that it is only a few of us who can say it whilst we are out of the country Zimbabwe.

The observer sometimes is a bit harsh on certain issues because she was young and saw some of the political situations. I feel sad; I have a wound which no one will heal because we have lost a beautiful country out of greediness and selfishness. Why is it that we want to be different from the rest of the world? What is so special about us when in fact we cannot even afford to feed our own people? Why are we no more accommodative were has the hospitalities gone where had the love their neighbours gone? Why are people no more respecting the human nature? The observer would like to ask a few questions to anyone who is prepared to answer him or her. Well in all the truthfulness kindness, in god's name is that what people of Zimbabwe went to the war to fight for? Why did we not just carryout a decree of understanding signed between the Rhodesian government and the majority people of Zimbabwe that were against oppression and served bloodshed and lives of people? It is rather a painful thing for anyone who is observant as the observer herself.

This war brought many lies than the truth of the matter the death of certain leaders was it timed or just unlucky or a mystery that nobody will ever tell the people of Zimbabwe the truth of the matter. Tongogara, it's not easy to forget him , if only, if only he was here, it's rather too emotional to think he is not talked about, I think he is the war hero of Zimbabwe and should have had a monument put up in Harare, and people celebrate Tongogara Day. He was the main man when it came to the gorilla training. His death puzzled a lot of people. If he had been here today maybe he could have saved the people of Zimbabwe, from all the atrocities that they have suffered.

The country that people died for is now a country of lawlessness, very poor, rather considered the poorest on earth. Corruption is more of a norm. Talk of instilling fear and intimidation, since this was experienced during the Rhodesian period why are black people suffering the same consequences in Zimbabwe this day and age? Firstly it was the Rhodesian government which instilled fear and intimidation to black people of Rhodesia then now it is the Zimbabwean black government instilling fear and intimidation to its own people. I ask myself most of the time did we break away from the past or was the past better than the future? What is going on? Do not ask me I am as confused as you are. Mentally!

ZIMBABWEAN PERIOD

MAJORITY RULE: HOPES FOR THE PEOPLE OF ZIMBABWE

Recapture of the economic events. My experiences take me back when Rhodesia (then Zimbabwe) was a country which was habitable and full of life, and economically we were there trading with the international fraternity. Rhodesia was the breadbasket of Southern Africa. Rhodesia produced basic products like maize, wheat, sugar beans sorghum, grapes, hops and tobacco for our surrounding neighbouring countries. Rhodesia sold agricultural products, minerals on the international market. We participated on the agricultural shows, in Africa and Europe. The European Union had an agreement on our beef to be produced and cater for the European community. It was a pride of our country. The famous Harare Agricultural Show was an event not to be missed every year in August. The farmers had horse show jumping, paraded cattle like the African Zebu are used as draught oxen, as dairy cattle and as beef cattle, as well as for by-products such as hides, dung for fuel and manure, and other new cross breeds of cattle from overseas. The heavy industrial sector displayed their new technologies and machinery. Other industries had their new products displayed and demonstrated, from new types of foods to new kitchen gadgets. For those companies that had performed well, had maximized their profits nationally and internationally got a recognition award from the minister of trade and commerce. Long term service employees were also recognized and awarded medals.

After independence, when the country was now being ruled by the majority people, it was welcomed with open arms. The excitement was overwhelming. At last we have a black majority rule in Zimbabwe, everybody is free, democracy has finally knocked on the majority people of Zimbabwe. All other countries in Africa, the international fraternity send their complimentary comments. Some were invited to the state banquet for the inauguration of the black majority rule. The British were given back their union jack flag which Lord Somme's and Prince Charles received took back to England. Lord Soames's was not interested in what was going on by the look of it. A lot of Zimbabwean portrayed him as the man who enjoyed the bottle for breakfast, lunch and dinner, which meant he was always drunk. But at least the inauguration went on well, we got what we wanted. We were able to go to places that we were not allowed we had the jobs that we never dreamed of having. But now we are rated the most corrupt country in the whole world? I will try to put you in picture later but firstly let me clarify a few issues.

We had in Zimbabwe the non-governmental organization coming in to help us to develop our country. We had pit toilets built they were very hygienic; we had boreholes sunken people had clean water for their household use. The non-governmental organizations came up with the introduction of using cow dung to create a gas for the rural use instead of cutting down the trees; we were going green by then. This was a way of trying to preserve the rural natural resources. The rural population understood the natural conservation of trees and the fact that they gave them fresh air.

There were rural based health care assistant who were send for training on basic first aid, medication administering, malaria prevention, and diarrhoea, and other tropical diseases some of them were usually the midwives for the village they worked hand in hand with the elderly woman for assistance in giving birth following our cultural values and the new methods that they were being taught. What to do in case of complications, in pregnancy. Every village town centre had a rural hospital to facilitate for medical emergencies for the surrounding villages' people. Everything was hunky dory that time. We enjoyed going to the Tribal Trust Lands because we could watch television due to the introduction of solar panels. People were happy that the war was over they were focusing on learning to live together with the white minority. Some of the white minority were not prepared to integrate so they left the country. Those who remained with time they understood that we needed to live together. I suppose on both sides was that the best preparation for the uncertain tomorrow was based on the fulfilment of the certain. We had to live together, period!

There were people like Eric Block, the economist. I respect the man who had already established a good relationship with blacks; he had no problems of interacting with fellow Zimbabweans. He was the presenter of the High School's quiz which was sponsored by Old Mutual Insurance Company. You would not want to miss his television program which was very educative and informative. It helped many high schools to do better and they wanted to participate in high school quiz and wanted to put their school on the map that it was the best. High school in Zimbabwe and parents would want their children to study there. Schools like Prince Edward, Convent Girls boarding and day high, Arundel, Chinhoyi, Marlborough, Glen Eagle Primary and High and others, in Bulawayo there were Fletcher high, Founder, Christian Brothers College, Evelyn Girls, Montrose, Townsend, North Lea, Falcon College, and Plum Tree high these were rated as the best high schools in Zimbabwe. These schools and many more competed to win the high school quiz every year.

There were so many people whom we miss, like Simon Parkinson's morning show on radio 3 in the morning was welcomed by most people of Zimbabwe. We had it all, my friends, we had it, in the land of milk and honey, Zimbabwe motherland. James Maridhadhi had a lot on his radio programs that most Zimbabweans would not miss for the world, especially his music programs that included music from overseas. Patrick Bhajila, Dominic Mhizha, James Maridhadhi, Tsitsi Mawarire Barny Mupariwa, Justine Mukoko, James Maridhadhi just to name a few were the nations favourite radio and television broadcasters. James Maridhadhi was very popular on his radio show for children, aged six to ten year olds. It was a phoning in program, that children shared their day's activities with the broadcaster; it was full of humour and fun, family secrets were revealed, he played their favourite song after the interview. James Maridhadhi took over after Mbuya Chirambakusakara retired. He was a hero to every six to ten year olds.

On (ZTV) Zimbabwe Television, we had many African dramas which were acted following the actual living way of our Zimbabwean family setup and some had such a lot of humour that you would laugh until you drop. Musically, we were kept in touch with the international music by John Matinde that was on television every Saturday evening, "Sounds on Saturday". This kept many kids off the streets. I remember that as a family we used to have our supper early on Saturday, do the washing up, prepared soft drinks, popcorn for snacking whilst we watched the Saturday family favourite programs like sounds on Saturday. We had a life in Zimbabwe life was going on well. All I have to do is to look back, reflect and with a bit of a tears in my eyes. I hope that one day the political and economic status changes, sometimes I feel like, it's only a Dream. No one makes you inferior without your consent. I do not know how other people of Zimbabwe feel because I feel I was robbed my freedom to enjoy the Mother Nature fruits of Zimbabwe. I feel I was used as a ritual sacrifice for the benefit of the others. If only I was sacrificed for something better I would not be here and feeling as guilt as I feel right now. In any case, I was treated like a pig which roasted itself in its own fat. Everybody who walks on earth has an excuse for their behaviour. There is continual shifting of balance between good and bad within each of us and in the external world. What is scary is that, bad winning. There is a sense of despair in the world. News footage of terrible wars, violence, crime, the horrors of disease and famine, all the global catastrophes, as long as these things do not touch our personal lives, we do not care. Most people are caught up in their own lives and their own problems. We dissociate ourselves from pain, strife, and the lives of others. I think in times gone past, we needed each other more. Helping each other was a more normal and instinctive way of life. These days, we view other people's problems, as theirs. It is easy to think in simplistic terms of someone being a bad person, and a nun being a good person, but these are just extremes. All actions in between the ordinary mundane ones count as well". "We are all accountable for the choices that we make. However, nobody and no action are beyond redemption. The difference between someone who has strayed down the wrong path and someone who is truly evil is that evil has no sense of remorse, never feels sorry.

Zimbabweans we are now scattered all over the world and some are even saying I will never go back to Zimbabwe again. I do say that as well but however, I believe that you are not supposed to say never in your life. I do not think that it is practical; anyone who migrated to Europe was hoping to spend a few years in Europe, work and earn some money, I bet it was specifically for just a short time, and then go back to Zimbabwe. People were not affording the basic necessities of everyday needs. But alas as the economy of Zimbabwe kept on deteriorating people including myself had high hopes, believed it will come to pass. The economy somehow was going to change for the better. We hoped for a code of understanding between the political parties. A miracle is what everybody hoped for. Nobody ever thought that the British were just going to be silent with the influx of foreigners especially from Zimbabweans coming to the United Kingdom. No hard feeling about that we have the same culture. Moreover, since some of us we were born during the Rhodesian period.

It's that time again; I have been in England for ten years, reflection time. We are now able to support our families at home. They are able to buy those things which were out of reach for some of us whilst in Zimbabwe. We definitely believe we will get there one day if ever there will be solution to resolve the problem of the economy of Zimbabwe the political status and be able to pay all the country's debts. I do consider that we are the unsung heroes in this country because there isn't very much being talked about us, we work very hard we do the dirty work that I think some people will never attempt to do.

Zimbabwe's economy was and is naturally based on agricultural production and mining. We used to enjoy watching the Zimbabwe Broadcasting Corporation when they used to announce the Gross Domestic Products (GDP) exports how much tobacco and minerals was sold on the international market, how much foreign currency generated for the country. It was a pleasure to watch the television and appreciate that the commercial farmers were doing a great job in order to keep the economy of the country stable, growing and able to sustain the people of Zimbabwe.

We were there when the prominent black business people started to set up businesses like the tobacco floors which were now built by some prominent people and we could watch the sales on television. It was uplifting to watch a black man owning big companies. There were quite a number of black prominent businessmen and women who were doing well in the development of new businesses or taking over from a white Zimbabwean It was a dream come true for others, and commiserations for others. However the margins of people's life style started showing, the poor were getting poorer, and the rich were getting richer.

Personal confession, I remember I went to the polling station were people were casting their votes, because my mother asked me to go. I did go but when I was in the queue I changed my mind turned walked back home and told my mother I had voted, what a lie, I never voted in Zimbabwe all my life. It is amazing, how I have managed to keep this secret for thirty-something years. I did not feel there was any need for me to vote. If ever she is going to find out she will wonder, but she would not be surprised. The thing was I did not trust what was going on I suppose I was very sceptic. The other issue was that I had a cousin, (the late) who came back from the bush war. The teaching that they had learned whilst fighting in the bush, did put me off. Because it was like holiday everyday there was nothing constructive, no direction, or future planning or organizing their life or going back to school or colleges to acquire skills. He believed that they were going to be staying in the white owned houses, and other political concepts that were so unbecoming like having gatherings, eating and drinking instead of going to look for work. He never believed that he needed to work harder than before to help develop our country.

Nowadays Zimbabwe's major towns are divided into two parts: one side people are throwing food away; the other side people are suffering unemployed and very, very poor. Nowadays the economic setup has separated people just like the rest of the world. A good example is the Sam Levy's in Borrowdale, Harare, Zimbabwe. Those areas are for the rich people; if you talk of starvation they look at you as if you have a problem with the political setup of the country. Moreover you are just a concerned citizen of Zimbabwe with an open-mind about the well-being and welfare of the human nature. Just showing the sentiment that you are a person who is worried about the welfare of your fellow citizens of Zimbabwe, to put this into perspective these are the majority of people who voted for this government to be in power. No one has their socio-economic problems at heart; people are now seen as political problems to the sovereignty of Zimbabwe. When they try to take their problems into the streets of Harare, and demonstrate, they are beaten or arrested and mostly maimed for life.

CONCLUSION

I have written this book in general, most of the other parts of this book are based on my reading and research that I thought might help you understand my country better. Some other issues I have personalised them due to the fact that they affected me and certain events, issues that I think were misleading to the people of Zimbabwe, this is my personal opinion. Reading has also helped me to research a lot about the pre-Rhodesian period, Rhodesian period and the present government of Zimbabwe. Zimbabwean government was supposed to implement the rightful law and order of our country. Nevertheless the Zimbabwean government has a high rate in violation of human rights. I am emotional to a number of issues, as to why they let people; "the so called people of Zimbabwe", built houses first then send bulldozers to destroy the houses.

Most of these issues were used as political instruments to demoralise the people living in the urban areas of major towns. It is just like oh! Wow! The government has done it again; wrong timing. Some people bought the land designated for building houses others were allocated according to the city council land allocation. Zimbabwean government has shown two sides of its decision making one it is for the people as and when they are in good books with the government, and it goes against them when they go against its policies. Following the long term town planning for Harare for years it has had plans of growing into bigger towns. The water and sewage systems in the major towns were already in for expansion. Creation of accommodation for all had to be planned. I still remember the railway line which was planned to be laid from Harare town centre to Chitungwiza. Where did that government plan go? There were many plans for the towns. However people of Zimbabwe never asked or voiced their concerns they were too scared. But the Zimbabwe government doomed their dreams. Most of the MDC's strong supporters lived in major towns. This party proved to be powerful, well-balanced opposition the Zimbabwean government.

This book is based on my ten+-year diary that I have been writing, recording how I felt about everyday events that I read from the newspapers, from 1980 to the present, especially the political, economic situation of Zimbabwe. However, many people I met were very interested to hear the political and economic status of Zimbabwe. They also encouraged me to write this book about my country. Some of them did not know my country, some did. I researched some of the material that I used to write this book. My views, how I feel, became interesting to read they thought it would be interesting to other people who do not know about my country and those who were born after the independence of Zimbabwe, "the so called born free". I hope everybody who is going to read this book will enjoy it. I feel that I have expressed some of my emotions, as much as I still cry sometimes, thinking about my beloved country. I wonder if it was not for the political and economic problems of Zimbabwe, where on earth would our beloved country Zimbabwe be economically and politically.

Last but not least, to all those disillusioned people of the sovereignty of Zimbabwe, heard that saying," Him to be, whatever your labours and aspirations, in the noisy confusion of life keep peace with your soul. With all its sham, drudgery and broken dreams it is still a beautiful world". Be careful. Strive to be happy, respect human nature, let us live, love one another. Just think of it, if there were no demarcations in this whole world, we did not belong to anybody; we could have been living in harmony. It is only a wish and hope that the next generation will learn to live in harmony. So far, there are enough problems to cover the whole world. "Christianity has not been tried and found wanting; it has been found difficult and not tried". We rather seek refuge in our comfort zones of other solitude bodies. This is my very personal opinion.

As an observer from afar, I do not look for elements that are combustible that will create fire if you rub them together. I suppose I am interested in the social structure within a given society, the set-up of a multi-cultural society. The world is changing and if you look at the margins you will find minority groups who have to bear the stigmata of the majority groups. I could not have hoped for anything better. The main reason I felt compelled to continue in prose was that I found it easier to describe certain political situation due to being there whilst it happened also as they involved me personally. Being in Europe is not easy, come rain come sunshine, home is always the best. But! But!

To everyone who is going to read this book I would like you to understand that after what happened to me, my experiences have led me to carry out research in anything that concerns Zimbabwe. Due to wanting the truth and finding out why we treat each other badly sometimes. It seems history repeats itself some we have inherited the evilness from our ancestors. Others are the ones who can help their fellow citizens with all their hearts; they are always there for you when you need them.

In this case my research my personal interests have gone beyond my expectations. I have been trying to deliberate some of my sentiments about the dreams which were shattered but eventually this book has made me discover some sensitive issues, violation of human rights at its best. As for the future generation of Zimbabwe I would like them to read and understand the atrocities that were suffered by the people of Zimbabwe. My dear friends "We lived, enjoyed the Rhodesian period and part of the Zimbabwean period". Why I said this, I do not know, see you later in my next issue, "Too hot to handle"!

God bless all those Zimbabweans who are scattered across the whole world, colour, race or creed you are Zimbabweans! Be proud to be one! Good luck!

Rate this book on our website!

www.novum-publishing.co.uk

The author

With a degree in agricultural economics and farm management, Paidamoyo Phillipa Jackson is a lecturer with a love of history and teaching. This is her first book and in it she conveys her personal journey, both physical and spiritual as well as her country's journey. It is based on her life, however it is not about the pivotal life experiences, or her immense courage through her journey, but more a record of her experiences for posterity. Her interest in the political, social and philosophical issues that led to Zimbabwe's complete collapse can be seen firsthand in this book where she discusses them emotively, passionately and extremely rationally. Paidamoyo Phillipa has two sons and dedicates her book to her mother and her late father.

novum PUBLISHER FOR NEW AUTHORS

The publisher

> *He who stops getting better stops being good.*

This is the motto of novum publishing, and our focus is on finding new manuscripts, publishing them and offering long-term support to the authors.
Our publishing house was founded in 1997, and since then it has become THE expert for new authors and has won numerous awards.

Our editorial team will peruse each manuscript within a few weeks free of charge and without obligation.

You will find more information about
novum publishing and our books on the internet:

w w w . n o v u m - p u b l i s h i n g . c o . u k